SO-ATX-006

"Trac

who understands the strengths women bring to the world and the barriers that women face exercising them. Her words combine both heart and head and are fresh, inspirational and enlightening."

MAUREEN F. FITZGERALD
PhD, JD, LLM, BComm., author, founder of FeminineIntelligence.com

....

"Tracy delights and inspires with her unique insights into the world of women and money. No matter where you are on the wealth spectrum, this book will help you feel more confident and at ease with your money. Tracy's conviction that women have more financial power than they realize will uplift and propel you into a radically new relationship with your money."

KARIN MIZGALA AND SHEILA WALKINGTON
authors of Unstuck: How to Get Out of Your Money Rut and
Start Living the Life You Want and co-founders of the Women's
Financial Learning Centre and Money Coaches Canada

....

"The power that comes from listening to Tracy is both immense and rewarding. We all stand a little taller and a great deal stronger as a result of listening to her."

DEBORAH TWOCOCK
executive director, Dress for Success,
co-organizer, Sophia Wealth Academy

//////////////

Everything You
Really
Want to Know
About
Your Money

\\\\\\\\\\\\\\\

TRACY THEEMES

THE
FINANCIALLY
EMPOWERED
WOMAN

FIVE STEP FINANCIAL

PLANNING GUIDE

LifeTree
MEDIA

Published by
LifeTree Media Ltd.
www.lifetreemedia.com

Distributed by
Greystone Books Ltd.
www.greystonebooks.com

Tracy Theemes, MA, CFP, FMA, FCSI
Financial Advisor
Sophia Financial Group
Raymond James Ltd.
3762 West 10th Avenue, Vancouver, BC   V6R 2G4
t: 604 569 2891
f: 604 222 5488
tracy@sophiafinancial.ca
www.sophiafinancial.ca

Cataloguing data available from Library and Archives Canada
ISBN 978-1-928055-00-6 (paperback)
ISBN 978-1-928055-02-0 (epub)
ISBN 978-1-928055-1-3 (pdf)

Editing by Sylvia Taylor and Maggie Langrick
Cover and interior design by Jessica Sullivan
Printed and bound in Canada by Friesens

LifeTree Media Ltd. is committed to reducing the consumption of old-growth forests in the books it publishes. This book is one step towards that goal.

To my mom, Bonnie Theemes—truly
the best mother and mentor a woman could ask for

AND

To my "Aunt" Helen Girardin,
who has been like a second mother to me

These two amazing women "bookended" me my entire life. They told me I could achieve anything, make the world a better place, stand up for truth, protect the vulnerable and still have the napkins match the table motif. Most importantly, they taught me to laugh my guts out no matter where I was and that I was worthy and lovable. I have been truly blessed.

CONTENTS

ACKNOWLEDGMENTS

MY GRATITUDE goes out to the legions of women who have come through "snow and rain and heat and gloom of night" both literally and figuratively to learn about their finances. You are a brave, hardy and inspiring lot, and I have been changed by your stories and acts of courage.

I am truly grateful to our clients. These men and women have decided to move through the fire of their own uncertainties and the cacophony of voices around them to bring clarity and purpose to their financial lives, and I am honoured to share the journey with them.

Heartfelt thanks to my brave, powerful and brilliant business partner, Kamal (I've-got-your-back) Basra. What a woman!

There would be no book without Sylvia Taylor, my ever-optimistic editor and advisor, who never lost her patience or sense of humour. Thank you. My other muse, Marial Shea, kept me going when the going got rough. And Maggie Langrick, you are a knight in shining armour, riding up just in time to save the damsel in distress. I treasure your wisdom, encouragement and advice. They are gifts for which I will be forever grateful.

Bless the hearts of the legions of readers at Raymond James in the compliance, financial planning and marketing

xii · *The Financially Empowered Woman*

departments, whose job it was to make sure I wouldn't cause irreparable damage to their reputation or get thrown in jail. I believe that task was accomplished.

I am also thankful to the teachers, friends and supporters—and even the detractors—along the way who have passed on their wisdom and sometimes even their foolishness for the purpose of helping me to become the best financial advisor I could be. Special mention goes to Kirk Otto, Jeanne Denning and the incredible Gloria "tits up" Strait, who kept me away from the minefields in my first years on the job. Special thanks to Karin Mizgala and Sheila Walkington, my professional "homies."

Where would I be without my sisterfriends (yes, it is one word): Mary Lynn Anderson (the other "Queen Street Girl done good"); Marlene Delanghe and Jo-Anne Lauzer, my double home team advantage; and Angiola-Patrizia (where-have-you-been-all-my-life) DeStefanis. And I am so grateful for Sony Baron, Bev Pugh, Carrie Gallant (my mental health squad); the colourful Christine Scaman; and my dear woman Donna Soules, whose role in my life defies earthly description. My deepest appreciation to (and of) Super Power Kirsten Severson, the most popular, courageous and beloved hermit you could ever meet, and the Fabs (past and present).

My heartfelt thanks to Michelle Pockey, who reminds me constantly that anything is possible when conviction is paired with action. What a mentor you have been and continue to be!

And in the spirit of last but most definitely not least, I want to acknowledge the support and encouragement of my small but mighty family: Todd (best brother in the world, even though he still doesn't think I'm funny); Rob and Elizabeth; Charlie and Aunt Roberta. You may not be "the wind beneath my wings" (I don't like heights anyway), but you are most assuredly the earth under my boots. Or in Vancouver lingo, the umbrella in any rainstorm. Love you dearly!

FOREWORD

I FIRST MET Tracy Theemes in 2008, at a downtown coffee shop in Vancouver. We were both investment advisors for large bank-owned brokerage firms in Canada. Several people had suggested that we should get to know each other. I only knew her name and that she was doing educational investment and financial planning seminars for women, similar to what I was offering.

I saw a smart, attractive woman with a gentle elegance and grace, and when she spoke, the words came from a place of deep knowing and confidence. When she smiled, her eyes lit up and one sensed that she was very comfortable in her skin and possessed a groundedness that I had not seen in very many people before, especially in our industry. I liked her immediately.

We began talking and very quickly realized how many things we had in common. We were both midlife women with extensive financial and life experience, we each had two teenaged children and we were working in an industry that did not seem to understand us as advisors nor as clients. We didn't quite fit.

Growing up, we had witnessed women struggling to get ahead in society. Some of the struggles had to do with lack of education and resources, but others were because of external societal structures that made it more difficult for women to advance. Women struggle to maintain financial security while being the primary caregivers and are often out of the workforce for many years to take care of children and family members. We typically work part time at lower wages to balance our family responsibilities and still earn 70 cents for every dollar our male counterparts earn. Add to that the statistic that women live longer than men and that women tend to be more risk averse, and that leaves us in a very troubling scenario, where financial security becomes a challenge. This was our reality, and no one seemed to be talking about it.

Independently, Tracy and I had arrived at the same conclusion and shared the same perspective: In order to create a just and more equitable society, we needed more balance at the leadership levels. The views of half of society were not being represented or heard.

We both strongly believed that education and financial security were two of the foundational pieces required for more women to be able to step forward and increase their leadership roles in society. This belief laid the groundwork and forged the bond of our partnership with a very clear vision: to support women in becoming financially strong and independent, by providing high-quality education and expert financial advice. At the end of our meeting, we knew that something very unique had just happened and we had found a kindred soul in each other.

After a few more meetings, we decided to create our own company, Sophia Financial Group, named after the Greek goddess of wisdom, to stand apart in an industry that is often perceived as chaotic, random and tumultuous. Our path was clear—we would help women find and exercise their financial power so that they could contribute to creating a better world for everyone.

As I got to know Tracy, I realized her strength was not only in providing sophisticated investment advice and portfolio management skills; her background in psychology brought with it extensive knowledge and scientific research on the differences between the male and female brains, differences in how we process information and how we perceive the world. This, in conjunction with her research background on gender and finance, provided a component that would set us apart in our industry.

Tracy decided something needed to be done to expose the real truth about women and money, and this became the basis for her seminars. She developed Sophia Wealth Academy for Women as an annual event to help women gain the tools they needed to start making smart money decisions.

Ever-increasing demand for her seminars confirmed that women need to have a resource, a safe place where they can ask any and all questions related to money without fear of judgment or shame. This is what led to her writing this book: She wanted to offer a handbook, a resource, a starting point, for any woman who feels frustrated about money and wants to learn more so that she can build a solid foundation for herself and her family.

Just as we have witnessed women's struggles around money, we have also been very fortunate to witness women become strong and empowered and take control of their money to create the life they want.

Women can change their relationship to money, one step at a time, methodically and with wisdom. Anyone can accomplish this. We know. We have seen it happen. It can start now.

KAMAL BASRA, CFP, FMA, FCSI
Financial Advisor
Co-founder Sophia Financial Group, Raymond James

INTRODUCTION

WHY DID I WRITE THIS BOOK?

This isn't a book about investment or portfolio optimization, or a how-to book on buying low and selling high. This book is about supporting women to become owners of their financial lives.

Cynicism and fear are pervasive in our culture, and I understand how this can create a threatening environment for a woman and her money. So many women say they don't know enough or don't have enough, and they become too fearful to take the reins. I watch them throw up their hands and say, "To heck with it, ignorance is less stressful. I'm outta here!" I can sympathize with this sense of being overwhelmed.

I want you to know that you are not alone, that you have friends with you on the journey to financial empowerment. That this journey is manageable and that you are as capable and intelligent as you need to be to manage your money and make it work for you. You don't need to have been born with a passion for numbers or the steely nerves of a high-stakes Vegas gambler. You just need some information, delivered in a way that makes sense and feels relevant to you, and the confidence to use it.

Many women approach financial management with an all-or-nothing mentality: either we let someone else handle all of it for us, and hope for the best, or we think we have to run everything ourselves.

We have so many conflicting roles and expectations to juggle. We think being responsible means trying to do everything ourselves. And this can get us into trouble. Most of the time it isn't necessary, or even desirable. I don't think everyone who needs a tune-up needs to learn how the engine works. My belief is we should have a maintenance schedule and know a good mechanic. We just need to know enough language to communicate about what is making funny noises and have the ability to determine if the job got done. Financial control exists along a continuum, and there's a broad, safe middle ground between total independence and blind delegation.

Our financial processes must fit our lives. If managing money continues to be based on men's sociological, economic, linguistic and cognitive predilections, it's going to continue to feel inauthentic, and even daunting, for us to try to fit into those paradigms. We are going to continue to feel like imposters and uninvited guests. And if investing and financial planning feels disconnected from the things we love and care about, it's not going to work. We will feel lonely, cut off, angry, discouraged and unable to pinpoint the source of our discomfort.

This book is also about helping you figure out what you need and don't need to know, and what you need and don't need to do. One of the hardest tasks of taking control of your own financial situation is discovering what you do and don't care about and pinpointing the areas in which you are under-informed and full of trepidation. Armed with that self-awareness, we can bring the aspects of your economic life that most matter to you into the light.

Maybe you'll even discover why you feel a certain way about money and that others feel that way too. You will come to understand the psychology that lurks behind the feelings. You'll find out how others coped with the same frustrations and learn what worked for them. Some of the same solutions will work in your life too, helping you to move more efficiently and easily to your next step.

This book is about helping women know what questions to ask, how to ask them and where to find the answers. But mostly, it's about being on a journey, sharing what works so that we can be smarter and wiser in the steps we take, while creating a sense of well-being about the process. I want you to know that you are connected to all the other women who are out there—moving along the path, sharing some laughs, maybe a couple of tears, as we put one foot in front of the other and encourage each other to keep going.

Whether you are a single mother on welfare, a recent divorcee or a multi-millionaire, I believe it is your birthright to maximize your potential, put your financial house in order and step into your own financial empowerment.

MY JOURNEY

//////////////////////

WHAT THE HECK IS A PSYCHOLOGIST DOING WORKING AS A FINANCIAL ADVISOR?

In my late twenties, I was doing doctoral work in child psychology and working as an infant development consultant in the gritty and troubled Downtown Eastside of Vancouver. Each of the families admitted into our program had at least two presenting issues (drug addicted mom with a child with Down Syndrome, or a baby born preterm into a family with a history of violence, for example.) These were most often families in high distress, facing a diverse mix of challenges.

In my last year there, three of the babies on my caseload died. I felt strongly that two of the deaths were triggered by economic factors. These tragedies were preventable. I believed that if those families had had enough money, the child's life would not have been lost. This realization led me to a huge spiritual crisis.

I just couldn't understand how in one city we could have such a contrast in human conditions. One child is taken to the doctor with a weight problem while six blocks away another child doesn't have enough to eat and goes to school hungry. It was like money was getting stuck in certain places and didn't flow evenly from one side of my city to the other.

I became fascinated by why some people were rich and some people were poor. It struck me that finding an answer to this question was even more fundamental to the well-being of my clients than understanding the human psyche or knowing whether to lay an infant on her back or side when sleeping. Everywhere I looked, people, communities, companies and even countries, seemed to be stressed out about money. And given that not having enough money was a potentially fatal situation, I began to appreciate the magnitude of this issue in our world.

I started to think a lot about money. I wondered how we could get the money to move from where it was in surplus to where it was in short supply. What could I do to ensure that resources got funnelled to where they were needed? What was my role in that? What is money anyway? Who gets it and who doesn't? And why are there so many problems around it?

I began to suspect that I wasn't going to be able to address these critical questions by traipsing around the streets of the Downtown Eastside with my toy bag and a developmental assessment inventory. The foundational issue that needed to be resolved wasn't about child development, outdoor play or whether a child's daycare was licensed. It was having the money to purchase what that child and family needed to function optimally.

I decided I wanted to help eradicate poverty (at least in my corner of the world, to start), and to do that, I had to understand money and how it worked. Ten years of post-secondary education had not prepared me for this undertaking. The path I was on no longer felt right. I left the doctoral program in child psychology that I had worked so hard for and decided the first place to learn about money was the business world. That was the start of my spiritual journey into the realm of money, leadership and power.

I found employment with an international play equipment company and went from the world of child psychology into sales. My former college mates and professors were aghast. My family was in a state of shock, and friends questioned my sanity. But what better way to take a cold plunge into economic waters than by having to sell something to earn your income? It was a horrible, exciting, discouraging and fascinating transition.

I was now awakened to the reality that it is the currency of money that makes the world turn. I had always thought that it was love, relationships or maybe even health. But I now saw that without money, you can't support any of those things. You can't eat. You have no accommodation. You have no clean bed for a child to sleep in.

This realization marked a major shift in my values.

As is common in most homes, I was raised with the vague sense that money was really *important* but was taught few specifics about what it is and how it works. The essence of money was mainly communicated through clichés like: "Money doesn't grow on trees" and "You think I'm made of money?"

I was fortunate to be raised in an entrepreneurial home. My parents ran a tree service business and several other ventures. My brothers and I accompanied our father after dinner while he did estimates for tree removal around the city. I helped my mom every week do the accounting and some of the marketing for the business. But no one ever taught me what money was really about, how to make it grow (or shrink!), its role in a successful life or the enormity of what we can do with it when it is well managed.

My "real" education about life was given in the home, about the home. I was taught how to wash clothes, to make decent brownies, to iron pleats and to do a tidy hospital corner on a bed. My mom did the best she could to prepare me for the life she led and understood. She stewarded the food in our fridge, served leftovers on Wednesdays, darned socks and re-soled shoes. We kept to our budget when buying groceries or looking for prom dresses. We carried coupons to the grocery store and kept a change jar for saving. She modelled the prudent and efficient management of a well-run home.

But managing the household budget is not financial empowerment. I came to see that real economic power is not about the pennies. It may start with the pennies and an understanding of cash flow, but it expands far beyond these matters. Economic power is about connecting to the principles of wealth and understanding how it works.

This is where my journey as a woman who wanted to master money and "grow up financially" got interesting.

For almost ten years, I moved through the ranks and was transferred to the U.S. with the international play equipment company I had left doctoral work to join. I later left that company to start my own business in the U.S. and then sold it. I was ready to move to the next level of financial questioning. I walked into my local Smith Barney office, a brokerage firm that is now owned by Morgan Stanley, and asked to speak to the branch manager. I explained that I was selling my business, was bored out of my mind and that the only thing I was really interested in was money. Did he have any career opportunities? He asked me to sit down. At that point, my money journey moved up to high gear.

At that time, Smith Barney helped two-thirds of the United States' penta-millionaires manage their investments. The company had been in business for over a hundred years. Wealth seemed to be embedded in the bricks. It was a phenomenal training ground and the most successful corporate culture and financially wealthy peer group I'd ever experienced. Everyone had money, talked about it, invested in it, played with it, made it work. I was coached, mentored, trained and molded.

I was drawn to the issue of women and investing and did extra research and training in that area. Smith Barney had already determined that women were the next tidal wave of investors and had set up a special department to study that phenomenon. They knew the demographics and collected cutting-edge research on how women think and behave around money. At that time, women were one of three projected areas of investor market growth in the U.S. (the other two being Puerto Ricans and gays.) It was one of the first firms to identify that women think about and handle money differently from men, and I was a beneficiary of that research.

The demographic that fuelled this intense interest showed that two-thirds of all assets in the U.S. and Canada were going to be owned by women by 2019. Smith Barney was trying to get a handle on what this might mean. Women weren't known as the primary financial decision makers, and the idea that they would become the majority stakeholders of the country's assets was at first just an interesting statistic, an opportunity to be exploited. Over time, the implications have become more confusing to the financial services world. First of all, the switch to predominantly female ownership isn't happening for the reasons you might hope: women were about to reach this status not by breaking through the glass ceiling or doing a great job running companies but because of the largest intergenerational transfer of wealth, followed by the largest intergender transfer, in history.

Because members of the prewar generation were savers, large amounts of inherited wealth are being passed on from one generation to the next. And because women are outliving men, a large percentage of that transfer will land in women's hands. But what women haven't fully understood is that this may be a one-generation opportunity only. They can either pass it back to the men for management, or they can do something with it that reflects their values, missions and objectives so that the world might be changed radically. Or not.

This opportunity to make a difference, to be of service to all humanity while learning about stocks and bonds, was utterly intoxicating. And it turned out that the study of financial markets was not as far removed from my educational background as I had originally thought. The study of wealth was fascinating to me. It is psychology on speed. Because money is controlled by humans (I sincerely hope it is, anyway), it is a rich ground for studying behaviour, decision-making, assumptions, belief systems and language. I examined the differences between people who had money and those who didn't, and immersed myself in looking at it from all sides of the wealth continuum, from multi-generation poverty to high-net-worth families. I leapt out of bed every morning ready to tackle the financial world, convinced that I was now in the heat of my own personal, financial and spiritual quest.

In 2005, I moved back home to Vancouver and began work with a large brokerage firm owned by one of the big banks. I found myself immersed in a pretty traditional (i.e., masculine) way of doing business. I was convinced that women investors wanted a different approach and would appreciate a full-service one-stop-shop approach where all the issues of their financial lives could be addressed. I believed that people wanted to be treated respectfully and given objective, wise advice about their whole lives and not sold a product just because it was the Hot Tip of the Day or had a high commission for the broker. People, women especially, wanted to discuss money in the context of their life journey and in terms that made sense. I was fortunate to then meet my incredible business partner, Kamal Basra, and Sophia Financial Group was born.

Kamal and I had seen empirical, concrete evidence that men and women tend to handle money differently, and we knew that women felt underserved and misunderstood by their advisors and the institutions they worked with. So much of what goes on at the top level of the financial world is still dominated by men—of a certain race and even of a certain age and lifestyle.

And with that come subtle, inherent and insidious assumptions, attitudes and behaviours.

We imagined offering a service in which the structure of the financial world could be translated into a language that is easier to understand, more relevant and more rewarding for the families we serve. The Sophia perspective is a holistic approach to financial well-being. We help women identify the role money plays in their own life, drawing in support from other sources where required. We encourage women to approach this process proactively, before some major life challenge propels them into it, because it's not just about money. It's about stepping up and taking control of your life.

We agreed that it was important to us to do one day per week of pro bono work, helping people who need high-quality advice but may not have access to it. This includes disadvantaged women, families in debt, new immigrants and refugees who need an orientation to our financial world. Our pro bono work also includes doing numerous education programs and presentations to groups that we identify as either needing the knowledge for themselves or that will use it to benefit others. Some of our work is counselling the emerging leaders of our community to get their own personal financial lives on track. We want them to have financial peace of mind so that they can do the work we can't, like running meal programs, teaching the young and protecting rainforests. We also believe that you probably shouldn't be running organizational budgets for others if your own financial world is in disarray.

ALL THOSE YEARS ago, when I first set out on my mission to figure out how to make money move, I would never have guessed that it meant becoming a financial advisor. But now I see how the pieces are coming together. The vision has become a reality. My psychology background has married my interest in finance, and the west and east sides of our city merge at Saturday morning classes at Sophia Wealth Academy. We are there encouraging, educating and supporting a new financial paradigm, with all of its challenges, rewards and blessings.

If a woman armed with a toy bag, a good hospital corner and the desire to make things better in a community can take on the financial world and become empowered, so can you.

OUR JOURNEY

////////////////////////////

EVERY WOMAN HAS A UNIQUE STARTING POINT

My mom used to say, "Everyone's on a different journey. If all of a sudden you look up and see a whole lot of people walking on the same path as you, someone has got it wrong!" She encouraged me to be an individual and to be okay with my unique life journey. Everyone can be travelling in the same direction, but we all have our own divine calling.

Money is the same way. The path of travel is an individual one. We might all hold the same map or even be going to the same destination, but the vehicle, speed, rest stops and roads we take are determined by our own distinct set of circumstances.

There are, however, patterns in what many of us have experienced in our upbringing. I have never yet had a woman tell me that when her mom sat her down at the age of twelve to talk about the "facts of life," her speech was, "Honey, in our family we believe in a 60-40 asset allocation strategy and are unimpressed with the benefits of currency hedging."

But we are often taught how to be attractive. We get instruction on how to apply eye makeup, which colours go with which others and how to style our hair. Our "facts of life" talk typically comes with warning labels about men, sex and hygiene. That is what my mother and her peers spent their time on. They taught us what we needed to know to run a home, raise functional children, keep a job and look nice.

Then each family imparted its own set of essential, idiosyncratic life skills. I got training about how to balance my cheque book, how to run a business and how to get the best price on a tree job (thanks to Dad for that.) Not too shabby for a woman of my generation. Your family toolbox probably looked quite different. Each of us ends up with a unique patchwork of skills and competencies, but many of us tend to lack a general knowledge of economic structures and how to operate within them.

Most women say that when they have to start making some of those larger decisions on their own for the first time, they have little experience, a warped frame of reference and, most importantly, the perception that they don't—and perhaps can't—know enough to make a confident decision. I hear this repeatedly. Lack of confidence is a common concern, and it significantly affects how women deal with money. This means we have to either get information from peers, figure out how to hire a set of advisors that we trust or learn in some other way so that we can get the confidence to make empowered decisions.

Many older women say that younger women are different today. They don't have the same issues and weren't raised with the same degree of pressure to be a certain kind of woman. I am not so sure of that. I recently spoke to a group of sorority sisters at a local university. It was a delightful experience. The events committee had done a survey on what topics were of interest to the members and had had a resounding response that the group was keenly interested in learning about finances. They were expecting hundreds of young women to attend. On my way out the door my business partner jokingly said, "You'll be lucky if there's 20 students there." We both chuckled. There were 35. And I was totally okay with that.

At one point during the presentation I could see that the energy was flagging. I looked up at the audience and pointed to a group of four students in the fifth row. I called out, "You girls! Why are you yawning?" Like the nice young women they were, they quickly found polite reasons like being in the middle of exams, it's been a long day and a variety of the "dog ate my homework" excuses.

I challenged them further. "I am not insulted. My feelings are not hurt. I am just curious: I know I am not boring. So, what is putting you to sleep?" Then they sat up and took notice. The whole room waited in anticipation. Who is this crazy presenter confronting us? They hemmed and hawed and finally one brave soul from the dark corners of the back of the room yelled out, "I just want to marry rich!" The room exploded in laughter. Appreciative laughter. I thanked her for saying what was on her mind and got even more curious. "What is that about? Tell me more." They could see in my face that I was alive with interest.

What followed was some of the most honest dialogue I have ever had. They told me how very stressed out they were, and said that marriage looked like an option that might relieve them of those burdens. They felt that they had a better chance of achieving financial success with a husband than on their own. We investigated the costs and benefits of this approach. I also wondered what they thought their parents were doing by sending them to college. Was this just a new form of "marriage mart"? They honestly weren't sure. I was fascinated.

A few weeks after the sorority experience I sat on a panel at an event for young women in business. The topic raised there was "cleavage and power." I told them about my friend Christine who likes to say, "The amount of a woman's breast that shows at any given time is directly proportionate to her lack of power." They disagreed ferociously.

It took four mature women on stage to handle their fierce assertion that wearing revealing clothing was a good way to get jobs and get noticed. We countered with "Noticed for what?" "What jobs are you talking about?" I am coming to the conclusion that young women in my community are conflicted about the messages they hear, the expectations they perceive about their worth, and are so stressed out from acting out a part, that they are willing to accept almost any kind of bargain that gets them out of this pressure cooker of competing expectations.

So, no, I don't think young women today are really very different from their mothers. (Although, of course, I think *they* think they are.) I was given a conflicted set of values to deal with, and so are they. The portrayals of women in the media are now alarmingly sexual, but I also had unreachable *Good Housekeeping* magazine standards to contend with, and Samantha from *Bewitched* and I *Dream of Jeannie* in her harem outfit on TV. The pressures might have increased, but they haven't really changed.

The women who have made the greatest leaps in financial empowerment are those who have had their marriages fail. Divorce can be the first time that a woman is forced to understand her money, and this is powered by necessity. There is also something to be said for anger as a motivator. It's amazing how quickly you can understand an investment portfolio or net worth statement when you are fuming. It often takes the experience of having hopes dashed and expectations shattered before some of us face the demons of our financial dependence. It is unfortunate that it takes such a shocking, negative situation to force our emancipation. We may have spent years relying on someone else to save us from financial responsibility. There has to be a darn good reason for us to go through the fires of this intense internal conflict. And it is hot in there!

Clearly, I don't think age is the determining factor that separates those who are on the money journey from those who are not. It is circumstance and, to some degree, an innate wisdom that keep some women out of the swamplands altogether. But many of us need to find our own way onto the path, and I am grateful for whatever it is that brings women to the point where they thirst for knowledge about finances.

No one is too old to learn about money. My favourite class attendee of all time was Sally, whom I met when I was working in Olympia, WA. She was 94 years old and would climb up four flights of stairs to get to the class. She took the same four-part series twice and had an impact on me and on everyone in the class. First, she was gorgeous, vital and unfailingly forthright. She was a role model for what 94 can be. Second, she imparted the kind of wisdom that you can only achieve with a long and fully experienced life. We had two 78-year-olds in our first class who kept complaining about how hard it was to learn the concepts of money at that late age. Sally told them in no uncertain terms that if she could do it, so could they. I remember a particularly meaningful exchange between her and a 28-year-old who was lamenting that if she went home and told her husband she wanted to look at the investments, he would get mad. She firmly straightened her out with, "I thought that with my first two husbands, honey, but it's just not worth it!" Sally took them to task in a way my 40-year-old self could not. And she did so bluntly, lovingly and with a gleam in her eyes that put an end to backtalk. I still think of her.

FINANCIAL EMPOWERMENT

Empowerment exists when a person owns their story and their life, inside and out.

To own your life is both overwhelming and intoxicating, because to start with, it is all about self: who you are, what you stand for and what you really need and want. I'm not asking you to stop caring about others. But the more deeply a woman is rooted in who she is, the more stable her journey and the more able she is to help the people she cares about. Some of us are more or less educated than others, some started out richer or poorer. There are a myriad of circumstances within a gender, but each of those stories has honour and dignity when we own it and say, "This is what I need," "This is what I care about." Owning your life helps you not freak out about things you're unsure of.

It's interesting to look at what we have trouble owning up to and what really moves us. I remember hearing an expert on the family say, "For a woman, her house is an extension of self. For a man, it is like a campsite." I found this both funny and annoying at the time. I know that when I watch women in their homes, I usually get the sense that they own them. They care about how the dishes are done, how the laundry gets sorted and which dish detergent gets used. Yesterday, I listened to a very bright young female business owner talk about detergent for almost five minutes. I looked over and saw clearly that her husband didn't care and wondered who would end up having ownership of the dishes.

When it comes to having people over for roast beef dinner on a Sunday evening, you can see that in most cases the woman "owns" that roast beef. Whether or not she considers herself a naturally gifted cook, there is often an element of pride attached to her ownership of the meal. She knows how she wants to put the roast in the pan, what temperature to put it in at, whether to lay it rump-side up or down and how to season it. All this is based on what she's been taught before, things she's seen and her certainty about how she wants things to look and to unfold. We want to achieve that same type of certainty with money.

When we own our own life, we can create our own "money theology." That is a highly personal and unique set of principles, strategies and beliefs. You may have strong spiritual beliefs about money as well. There's an interior set of tasks that needs to be tackled and later expressed in our life. The internal work of developing self-knowledge and understanding the psychological aspects of money create the platform on which to build financial empowerment.

A woman needs to be very secure to ward off the negative influence of a daily assault of the messages so pervasive in our culture that the world is "going to hell in a hand basket." A woman who has her own financial plan can stay grounded, because she understands her own circumstances and has a personal road map to her self-determined destination. As long as she's in control of and understands her financial life, she can stay rooted.

A huge part of financial empowerment is self-management. I don't know many people who are naturally wired to competently handle money. When I dissect the behaviour, thoughts and beliefs of financially successful people, I see a lot of self-management and self-mastery. They learn when to ignore their feelings, when to act on them, when to put things in place, when to reward and not reward themselves and, very importantly, how to wait.

I've never met an affluent person yet who hasn't mastered delayed gratification. It's one of the major muscles of wealth. One thing our society is big on, unfortunately, is the drive-through window approach to life: wanting everything right now. The energy of wealth is not about instant gratification. It's a lot of *slow* and *grow*. Success often means delaying a reward, sometimes for quite a long time, and managing your behaviour along the way.

My experience of the wealthy is that they have also learned to do things when no one else is doing them. They sell when everyone is buying and vice versa. They don't wait for a wave of approval or confirmation by the masses. To operate this way, you have to own your strategy fully.

Empowerment also means defining success and what it looks like to you. It can be an enormous relief to realize that your idea of nirvana is not like the next door neighbour's. When you look deep inside, you may realize quickly that you don't even want a new car or a trip to Hawaii. Success is a highly personal matter.

I had a great conversation with my teenagers after an awards ceremony at their high school a couple of years ago. I had spent a long evening watching young people receive their science and math awards, and frankly, they were some of the most socially awkward people you could ever lay your eyes on. I couldn't imagine them running a city or fighting for the rights of the unfortunate. They could barely get themselves across the stage! This inspired a rich discussion at home. I asked my kids what they thought success was, and after getting that pained look on their face (the one that says "there she goes again"), we identified that in our family, social competence was a very strong value. We agreed that our definition of success had a lot to do with people and our relationships with them and was not so much about being a chemistry whiz or collecting a bunch of accolades. In fact, this revelation allowed me to let go of some of my obsession with their grades. Success, even for a secondary school student, was not just about academic achievement. (They were perhaps too relieved by this, as it later turned out.)

Some of the happiest people describe success based on what they're willing and not willing to do. I had someone say to me, "I really wanted to be a poet," and then talk about how he made compromises over where and how he was going to live to support that. It affected his decision about owning a house because he didn't want a mortgage hanging over his head. He felt this would compromise his freedom to choose this vocation. So, instead of defining success as having a million dollars in the bank, he defined success as waking up every morning doing what he felt he was put on the earth to do. Happy people make conscious choices and then continually tweak them. The unhappiest people I see are those who don't do what it takes to become successful on their own terms, both in identifying what success is and then taking all the little steps and risks needed to get there.

You begin by recognizing your gifts and abilities and acknowledging your challenges and opportunities so that you can be the steward of your own life. People who own their lives are able to ask for what they want and tell others what they need. They can say, for example, "I don't need to know about stocks and bonds—that's your job. What I need to know is how I can keep my mother living in her house."

It's all about relaxing into this process, determining what you need and making the most of who you are. It's also a good idea to become comfortable with constantly reassessing or "auditing" what you know and defining what you want to learn as things change.

This doesn't have to be serious or stressful. When I got my makeup done by a professional, I was happy with it at the time. But a year later, after considering what was available in the market, my expanded budget for makeup and clothes, and my increased knowledge of myself, I decided I wanted to go to someone else for a different style. The new esthetician was diplomatic but definitely changed some things about how I looked, putting me more in alignment with where I was at that point in my life. With money, it's the same way. We all carry stuff around with us, but we have to open up our luggage and check out the contents from time to time to see if it all still fits.

Empowerment means knowing where you are and being at peace with it. Knowing deep inside that no matter what happens you're going to be okay and that you have the resources to deal with any situation. It means having the knowledge, the tools, the emotional intelligence and behaviour, the belief system and language, to be true to yourself and to know what money can do for you. Believing that money, well managed, can enable you to achieve your dreams is the fundamental principle of financial security.

You can use wealth as an expression of your values. You can distribute and utilize money in ways that honour who you are and still get the bills paid. If you master this ability and perform it repeatedly, you may even have some left over to save the world.

Ultimately, it comes down to power, and that's not something that often gets talked about. We may have associations with power that don't conjure up thoughts of Good Witch Glinda. When the women in my classes talk about power, they often look a bit angry. The first comments are quite mixed: "Power corrupts." "It's why our world is in such bad shape." "It's used to control people." Eventually, those statements get worked through, and the ideas expressed become more neutral. Deep inside, we know that power itself is not the problem; it's how it's used that makes the difference: the why and the when and with whom.

I also hear people say that power is not a feminine concept. There was a young man in one of my workshops last week who actually had the courage to articulate that idea. I asked him to define "feminine." He searched for the right words and tripped over himself, and I let him stew in it for a moment as he tried to explain his position. Poor lad. I did let him off the hook eventually. No point in traumatizing him.

Many women also hold the belief that it's rather "un-lady-like" (remember that expression?) to want power for ourselves. These concepts of the masculine and feminine and power and strength are in the air we breathe and water we swim in. We are so immersed in them that we barely perceive the profound effect these social constructs have on our lives.

The issue of power has to be addressed because power is the energetic underpinning of money. That's a mouthful, but it's the crux of the matter. Women tell me repeatedly that they "don't like money." They like what it buys, but they don't like "it." Yesterday, a group told me they "didn't like numbers." They would rather be with their family or friends or have a root canal than look at a sheet of figures. Many said they were happy to get married so that they could "share the burden with someone else."

Sharing a burden is fine. Handing over the reins of your life to the first person willing to take them—or worse, to a person unwilling or unable to hold them responsibly—is not.

A bank manager I know is fond of saying that there are two things men do in most households: barbecue and look after the money. Unfortunately, of these two jobs, barbecuing is the only wise one to delegate.

When we talk with women during their child-rearing years about taking financial control, they often feel that we're asking them to take on yet another thing—to fix their own car, so to speak—when they're already running a household and working a job. That's the point when they break down and cry.

When we add women's discomfort with power to the widely held idea that financial responsibility will mean more work for them, you can see why there is often an internal battle raging over money.

SO, HOW DO WE HANDLE THIS?

Many of us just close our eyes, give our power away and wish for the best. It's comfortable and sometimes the only solution we can come up with that saves us from going insane. The problem is that giving something away means taking it away from yourself. Whereas sharing something means you keep hold of it, while potentially expanding it.

If we want a better society and a better life for everyone, then we can't be giving power away, and we certainly can't be giving financial decision-making away. Rest assured, I know very few women who would say, "I want to be economically empowered so that I can destroy the world." Maybe you could do something heinous with massive power, but the women I encounter would generally choose not to. I find that many women are very comfortable with shared power. And this quality can be transformative at many levels.

The downside is that having to take on yet another responsibility can seem overwhelming. Everywhere I turn, it seems that someone is lecturing me about something. I need to floss my teeth or do my eye exercises or take time with my kids or do volunteer work or pet my dog or learn just five Italian words a day. It is one task after another, and every added thing is one more place for me to feel guilty about not being the Perfect Woman. I always seem to fall short. No matter how many accomplishments or how much experience, it feels like it's never good enough.

We are all so tired of being on the judgment treadmill. Sometimes the shame about what we have and haven't done can send us into despair and inertia. When we don't feel in control of our lives, our compassion, intelligence and power can leak away, and this shows up in our decision-making and outcomes.

But we really don't need someone telling us how to balance our full-to-bursting 90-hour work weeks of a job and raising kids. I believe that lectures about "balance" are an indirect and harmful form of criticism. "You're just not good enough, honey, just like you always suspected."

All this stirs up a lot of emotion. I keep a Kleenex box on my desk, and I have to replace it every couple of weeks. Of course, it isn't really the money that makes us cry. Most of us have a standard that we feel we have fallen short of. We hold a set of ideals of what a financially empowered woman looks and behaves like, and it's hard to measure up. I hear so much shame and guilt over the course of the week, I could cry myself.

THE MEANING OF MONEY

Money has no value until you attach value to it. Our biggest misunderstanding is in thinking it's a concrete entity. We can feel like money is "not working for us," but money can only work based on the decisions we make for ourselves. We understand this intuitively. We all want to get money working for us to support our goals, where we are the boss of it and not the other way around.

Money is a tool, an assistant, a means to an end. It's not an entity that should rule our lives. Money is neither the car nor the driver—it's the gas in the tank. You're the driver. You can go in a Volvo, a Mercedes, or a Rent-a-Wreck, but none of those cars goes anywhere without gas.

I use the example of throwing a loonie or dollar bill into the middle of an emu farm in the Punjab. Not knowing its value, the farmer may pick up the bill and use it to scrape some dirt off her hands or pocket the loonie to put under a wobbly table at home. The emu would look at the currency as emus do: with slight disinterest. Now if you throw a carrot into the middle of the same field, the emu eats it and the farmer picks up what is left and knows its intrinsic value. The carrot carries its own worth. The dollar had to be deciphered and meaning applied to it. Money does not carry its own meaning—it is only in defining how it can be used that its worth is discovered.

One of the key differences I see in how men and women look at money is that men often see money as a goal in itself. They love the numbers and will talk about it as if it is the sole desired outcome. Most women respond to the idea of money as a means to an end. If I ask a woman what money is for, she has no problem articulating the reasons she wants and needs money, and it's often about caring for someone or something. But if I start with the numbers, charts and graphs without the context, I can see the "curtain" coming down and the shutting off of her soul. The numbers themselves have little meaning. They are without context, so she goes on mental strike.

The numbers are actually the least of it. Even in my work as a financial advisor I rarely need a calculator throughout the day. Most of the hard decisions are made at the level of personal values. The first step in the planning process is to find out what is important to a person, and then we find the financial structures that support those goals. Once that's done, implementation is fairly straightforward.

If a woman doesn't understand what she's about, and how to get what she needs and wants, money will boss her around. The bank will boss her around. Everyone who seems to her to have more knowledge than she does will continue to boss her around. The tail will wag the dog forever. Without a unified and articulated value system, she won't be able to say, "Well no, that's not how I believe money should be. That's not what I want my money for." Until she has that authority, there's always going to be a sense of being uncertain and disconnected from the power of what money can do for her.

I was at a dinner meeting with a man who had just retired. He told a story about the process he went through to get a financial advisor that he *and* his wife could relate to. He described how he would begin each meeting with the advisor candidate by reinforcing this goal and stating that his wife would be making the ultimate choice of advisor. And every time, the candidate would direct the whole conversation to him anyway. So, who is at fault here? Why isn't the advisor honouring this simple request, and why isn't the woman standing up and saying, "Hello, I am over here"? I get frustrated with the advisors, and then with the woman for not demanding to be taken seriously and treated with respect.

Thinking, feeling, behaving, speaking and being with authenticity is the foundation of a financially empowered woman. We need to be awake to what we are. We need to consider our psychological state and our knowledge base before we take action. The most creative, personal and effective process is to get comfortable with the inner landscape and have that inform our outer actions.

THE MONEY RELATIONSHIP

//////////////////////////

THERE **ARE** essentially three major factors that affect our relationship with money: psychological, cognitive and behavioural. Almost all of our financial issues, opportunities and actions come down to some combination of these three.

MONEY PSYCHOLOGY

The first domain is **psychological** in nature: the attitudes, ideas, belief systems, experiences and emotions we have around money. These can be wired, or drilled into us by family and society, or they can be some wild mixture of our personality predispositions with all the variants of those factors.

The psychology of money is itself a course of study. There are now whole journals and university departments devoted to the study of a field called Behavioural Finance and Behavioural Economics. This field challenges the idea that has been held for decades: that the stock market was efficient at all times, that it gave consistent results based on economic value and that the people who invested in the market behaved rationally. (It took you guys that long to figure this out?) The study of Behavioural Finance uses terms such as "aversion to ambiguity," "attention anomalies" and "disjunction effect." Basically, all of this is to acknowledge that human beings use a complex set of non-rational and rational decision-making methodologies to make financial decisions. Just watch my friend Meg at Freedman Shoes justify a cowboy boot purchase to herself if you want to watch this concept in action.

We are not rational when it comes to money, and that's okay, as long as you have consciousness about how and why you are making your decisions. It is not really sensible to buy flowers or give money to charity either, but it's not unreasonable if you know what the values are that fuel that decision. It's when we're asleep at the wheel that our lives career out of control. It's being blind to our own psyche that causes problems.

Our families of origin and the communities in which we were raised have a huge impact on our assumptions and orientation about money. I was raised in a small farming community where being exceptional was considered a very undesirable quality. I was admonished constantly not to "get too big for your britches." I also saw that the wealthiest citizens left town to indulge in their money-fuelled adventures and didn't talk about money much. Even if you were feeling fantastic and had just won the lottery, when someone asked you how you were, you replied, "fair to middling." Being in the middle and not standing out was a strong value. Most folks worked very hard for their living, and this quality was celebrated above most others. To this day, I can hear my brother and his friends speak glowingly about the biggest idiots, as long as "they work hard."

The controversial author, researcher and photographer Masaru Emoto is best known for his claims that human consciousness has an effect on the molecular structure of water. He has also claimed in his most recent work that ideas and values are transmitted and carried in the DNA of humans from generation to generation. I wish his work had more scientific credibility, because the concepts are certainly in alignment with what

I have personally seen and experienced in my work. It does seem that wealth and poverty get passed down through the generations.

My mother strongly believed in the power of consciousness to affect people and events. Having been diagnosed with a terminal illness, she spent several hours each day in the last six months of her life meditating and praying to solve as many issues as she could so that she wouldn't pass them on to me and her beloved grandchildren. Even if there is no empirical evidence to support this idea, we have all certainly seen this dynamic operate in families. The ability to achieve financial success almost seems like it is an inherited trait.

I work with a woman who was born in a war-torn country. She used the phrase "We were always insufficient." She said that inflation was so out of control in her country, it was as though a paycheque for $100 dropped in value to $50 by the time she got it home. They never had enough money for anything, and they were always wanting. Insufficiency and desperation had become part of her internal culture. She now has a dangerous money paradigm that leads to debt and insecurity. If a person truly believes that it is all hopeless, they are going to make millions of conscious and unconscious decisions that support that belief. This woman exists in a low-grade money horror show, and I am not sure we will ever expunge this belief.

We may have to circumvent it and put in some checks and balances that "trick" this deeply held idea into submission. For instance, this would be the kind of person who needs automatic bill pay and savings accounts that she can't view. She might benefit from payroll deductions for RRSPs and extended medical coverage as well as other insurances. We would have to build up her ability to handle having extra money, which I call the capacity for surplus. Over time, we might be able to nurture a belief system that could ultimately benefit her. Or we will find ways around it.

We find this same dynamic in people who are raised in a family in which successive generations have lived in poverty. The ability to hold on to surplus is simply not there and having savings can be highly anxiety provoking. I have worked with this issue in hundreds of women, and it's a very tough one to tame. But thankfully, I have also come to the conclusion that every "shadow belief" has its light side. For instance, in my family of origin, hard work was a very strong value. As I mentioned earlier, I was raised doing sales calls with my father after supper. The shadow of this is that I am predisposed to working harder at things than I need to. I have trouble sitting still, and leisure time is fraught with tension for me. But the light side of this is that I can usually get to where I want to go by sheer effort. Having been raised on a diet of business ownership and risk taking, I love the world of business and thrive when dealing with its challenges, which has come in very handy.

People often think money issues are insurmountable, and some are indeed quite daunting. But I have come to the conclusion that there are solvable and unsolvable problems, and revocable and irrevocable solutions. It's very important to know the difference. If your husband loves another woman, there's not much that can be done about that. If you are short and want to be tall, there's probably not too much you can change about that either. But trying out a new job or moving to a new neighbourhood, well, those can create big changes, and the decision can be altered later. Having a limb removed is an irrevocable decision, but money is in the domain of the very solvable because it is always changeable—whether you want it to be or not!

If you are willing to engage honestly with yourself and to investigate the areas of shadow that you believe might be holding you back, there is no limit to what you can do, how far you can go, or how much you can change. I have watched people rebirth themselves and go from dire situations of debt and money trauma to peace and solvency. We have all heard the stories of people who have failed at two or maybe even three ventures before learning enough to create the next big break-through business. I would not be writing this book if I didn't have utter and complete faith in the human ability to control and change our own circumstances through bravery and the harnessing of strong desire.

THERE ARE TWO aspects of the psychology of money which people don't discuss much. They are in the realm of what I call the Soul Economy. The first is the concept of knowing when a certain amount of money is enough, and the other is the role that emotions play in our financial lives.

When is enough enough?

Lynn Twist, in her book *The Soul of Money*, delves deeply into the concept of sufficiency. It's not about excess or poverty. If everyone got just what they needed, there would easily be enough to go around. That's not communism; it's realism. A lot of our ideas are based on being cut off from others, but we're part of a great big world where a lot of people don't have enough money to eat and some have butlers for their dogs. Where are you going to fit in, and what are your responsibili-ties? These are soul-searching questions that get addressed as you travel along the continuum of wealth.

One of the deep wounds in the world is the idea that "I don't have enough" or "I'm not good enough." Although we may have a warm bed, clean air to breathe and clean drinking water, there's a real societal sense of insufficiency. Sufficiency is wealth and is as much psychological as it is monetary. Some multi-millionaires feel they never have enough, while some other individuals might have just $2,000 per month coming in and feel completely free and wealthy and that life is sweet.

This sense of financial security isn't really a numbers game much of the time. One couple I worked with simply didn't make enough to afford basics each month. If you do not have funds to cover food and shelter I would say you do not have enough. Now do I think we can work with this situation to get it to a place of "enough"? Of course! I spend one day each week working with these challenges.

One woman who was in my office a few months ago asked if she was doing something wrong or missing something because she was supporting five other people on $900 per month, after rent, and it just didn't seem to be quite enough. In my opinion, that woman had an amazing ingrained sense of sufficiency. I know I couldn't get through a single week with only $900 if I had five other people to support. I feel she should probably teach a course, because her survival management skills are excellent. I told her she wasn't doing anything wrong, but we did conclude that she needed more income to cover her current needs. We put her in touch with a career mentor to assist her in maximizing her talents in a better job with better pay to increase her quality of life.

So, how do we know when enough is enough?

The question can be broached in specific ways like "Can I retire when I'm 60?" Of course, that answer depends on how much monthly income is considered sufficient. Or "Do I have enough to take a year off work to travel the world?" This also depends on the circumstance of what that year looks like. Is it enough to stay in hostels and travel third class, or is enough more about first class hotels and not renting out your condo while you're gone? There are the pragmatics of what enough looks like and also the internal work of making peace with the concept of enough.

The most powerful source of sufficiency is an internal one. You can alter how you feel about enough from the inside. Even when you feel financially challenged, you can train your brain to recognize what you do have. "I have had enough food and clean water today." We're conditioned in this society to look at deficit—what we lack—all the time, which leads to compensa-tory, reactionary behaviours. The mindset of wealth begins and ends with a deep sense of sufficiency.

I myself have worked with the mantra "It's okay. It is what it is. I have enough. I am enough." I seriously confronted the whole concept of "good enough" last year when I was nomi-nated for a local business award. I balked. I told my business partner that I didn't believe in competition. It was a masculine paradigm. I said I didn't like that it might make other women feel bad. I talked to her about how it creates segregation and status. She just looked at me. She answered calmly that it was really about bringing more attention to our business and being rewarded for what we had already accomplished. She rationally pointed out that it was an excellent tool for marketing ourselves, and she felt quite strongly that I should accept. I finally said, "No, let's just wait until I am good enough and might have a shot at winning." She just shook her head and on her way out of the office looked back at me and, with a resigned and patient tone, said, "And by the way, you are good enough."

Well, that threw me for a loop. I couldn't stop thinking about it. It didn't take long to realize the deep-rooted nature of such a limiting belief. I began to open my eyes to the way that notion was operating in my life. I woke up to the constant messages of insufficiency I was telling myself. And this was coming from a person who works with these concepts in other people every day! The power of the inner dialogue is mind-boggling. I can tell you with complete candour that when I manage to gentle that voice with messages of adequacy and gratitude for who I am and what I have, I do feel rich. I can also tell you that when I feel rich from the deepest core of my being, I am rich. Try it.

This is not a recommendation to do affirmations. I am not such a big believer in those any more. I am concerned that from what I see, they create a kind of reactivity in behaviour and emotions. Your subconscious doesn't really believe it anyway, if there is too big a gap between what you are saying and what you are experiencing, so in addition to feeling poor, you feel like a liar! I am convinced that wild, hairy affirmations are not the path to financial serenity.

So, own "what is," but also hold the idea that it is enough. Enough for today. Enough maybe just for this moment. And then we begin the beautiful journey of stringing those moments and days together. What's enough is what we have right now. Maybe tomorrow we can stretch our capacity a bit further, maybe even run some numbers and make a different plan. But the place to lay our foundation is right here, right now, with what is.

Emotions and money

Another aspect of the psychology of money is the role of emotions. We have managed to calm ourselves with the "mantra of enough," and now we can dig a bit deeper into our feelings, and when it comes to a discussion about money, feelings are never far away.

So, when do our emotions come in? Whether you want them to or not, they come in when your values are being threatened or supported, or when some message you have believed in for your whole life gets activated and brought to the surface. They come in during particularly stressful life transitions like marriage, divorce, death or selling a business. They can assist us by guiding us towards what feels good and hopefully away from those things that are not in alignment with our values and goals.

Emotions are the window to our values and beliefs. They tell us when we are on or off track. We can be neutral, charged negatively or feeling good. The role of emotions is similar to numbers in that they are diagnostic. They tell you if there are things that need to be changed. Sometimes I can be anxious and it can still be positive. I can get a bit riled up when I am trying something new, speaking to a group that is expecting great things from me or even when I am facing a conflict with an associate or friend. With reflection, I can quickly determine that these feelings are not telling me that something is wrong but are indicating that I'm just doing something different, and it's okay. The goal really is to be happy as much of the time as we can, while still growing and taking on as many new adventures as possible.

My friend Hans Erik and I used to eat lunch at a soup place down the street from our office. A waitress worked there whom everyone loved, and we all tried to get seated in her section because she was unfailingly good natured and cheery. She would crack jokes and was known for singing loudly as she made her way through the aisles. But this woman looked like life had not been easy: grey complexion, gravelly smoker's voice. One day, Hans Erik pointed out to her that she was the favourite server in the place and asked about her positive demeanour and good humour. She looked at him and said, "I learned a long time ago, sweetie, happy feels better." That always stuck with me. She had made her happiness by a series of choices, and I'm fairly certain that she was also quite sincere in her enjoyment of her life.

Last month a woman asked me if it was "okay" to give up a business she was working on that was not profitable. I thought it was a very interesting and insightful question, and my response was to ask her how she felt and what the consequences would be. There wasn't a technically correct or incorrect answer. She was very brave to come in and talk about the feelings she was experiencing and all the people she thought were going to be disappointed if she gave up her business. To me, that was a very valuable discussion.

Your intuitions can guide you about your priorities, beliefs and the people in your life. If you don't like your banker or insurance broker or even massage therapist, you don't need to keep them. I always say that the members of your money team must be people whom you genuinely like and trust. Do you have to marry them? No. In my opinion, working with an advisor is one place where a woman is allowed to have full emotional rein. Emotion is always going to play a role in finances. I'm not going to say that women feel things more deeply than men; I just think they're generally more able to recognize and articulate those feelings. If your stomach goes into knots at the thought of a visit to your financial advisor, I think you should honour that response and look for a better relationship. If you can't be honest and feel safe with that person, you are not going to fully utilize the incredible benefit this relationship can provide you over a lifetime.

I think we need to use head over heart decision-making in anything to do with investments. Conversely, this seems to be the place where people most want to use their intuition. You can't use intuition when it comes to buying low and selling high or tax planning or setting up a laddered bond portfolio. Investing is a head game. To do it well requires a dispassionate data-driven approach. If your emotions are getting activated over whether to sell or buy, you have already lost the game.

Emotions can sometimes get in our way. If we're super-sensitive to how we feel about things all the time, it can make life a bit challenging. Insight is good, but being ruled by emotions can have serious consequences. When a woman's mental state is clouded by too much emotion, she is not in a great place to make life-affecting decisions. I recall speaking with a woman who was absolutely full of rage. Her anger seemed quite justified. Very bad things had been done to her. But whether we have a right to our rage or not, in the long-term perspective it's in our best interest to get a handle on our emotions. This becomes super-important when transitioning through divorce or family business conflict.

A good rule of thumb is to use your emotions when dealing with a self- or people-related issue, and learn to ignore them when you are making investment and financial strategy decisions.

Sony Baron is a gifted grief therapist and divorce coach who works with a lot of our clients. She stresses that it is crucial that a woman make financial decisions from an emotionally stable place and not from an anxious, grieving or angry state. The reason, she explains, is that our emotional reactions are expressed in the right side of the brain, while analytical thinking and decision-making are expressed in the left. You can't see things in balance if one is overrunning the other. And we all know that strong emotions like fear or grief bring us into a kind of bare bones cognitive functioning that can cloud our ability to think creatively or problem-solve effectively. The best decisions are made with the brain fully activated and with an appropriate level of respect given to emotions.

A certain level of detachment is critical when making important life decisions. We train ourselves for wealth by mastering emotional control. We can begin to identify our emotions by seeing how we react to the messages around us, which can become an avenue for insight and new ways of responding. Women rarely achieve financial success without emotional self-mastery.

One aspect of our modern world that challenges our emotions almost constantly is the relentless presence of TV, radio, news and social media. We are goaded into greed or fear responses by mass media on a daily basis. This barrage of information and misinformation can seriously work against us in trying to manage emotion while remaining awake in the world. The stories we are fed swing from wildly positive to wildly negative. That's what sells newspapers and magazines and gets us emotionally wound up. The job of most media is to get us to come back to them again and again to purchase their stories and buy into their perspectives. Provoking strong feelings in us is their job.

We need to develop some kind of inoculation against this emotional seesaw. It is very difficult to be a good investor while also paying attention to what's going on in the news on an hourly basis. I'm very concerned about people holding tight to the media maelstrom of negative stories and manipulative headlines. It's profoundly important to ground ourselves in our own values, goals, needs and desires so that we don't get swayed by the media into making irrational decisions. In fact, this is one diet that could work wonders: a media diet. Look at your media consumption and make a rational decision about to whom you will grant authority over your headspace, then limit your intake to them. There are sources of information that are more reliable and accurate than others. And there are certain shows and definitely some public figures that will take you off course and activate your emotions. So, why put yourself through it? Goodness knows my adrenals are under enough stress just dealing with my family life.

MONEY KNOWLEDGE

The second major area of our relationship to money is cognitive: our knowledge about money. What we know. What we don't know. What we don't know we don't know.

When my niece told me she had her first boyfriend, I said, "Oh my, this means we have to talk about sex." She said, "No, we don't; I already know everything." The truth is, she doesn't know what she doesn't know. We really needed to do a "sex audit." It can be quite daunting to figure out what you don't know. Sometimes we don't know what we don't know, but we do have an inkling about our level of knowledge. Maybe you only know that 100 pennies makes one dollar. Some people may know what a stock or bond is.

A huge component in reaching your financial goals is to have an idea of the questions you need to ask and have answered to get to your end point. When I ask, "Do you have a net worth statement?" a woman may need to start with being able to say, "I don't know how to answer that question." That's a first step in learning about yourself: being able to say what you know right now, and that can lead to what you don't know. Eventually, I'd like everyone to be able to answer comfortably all of the financial questions that fuel their life, but not knowing something and being able to say so is also a very good departure point.

A self-made businesswoman came in to see me. She is very intelligent, runs her own multinational business and has $14 million in investable assets. And she admitted to me that she didn't really know what an RRSP was. Just because you can use a term in a sentence doesn't mean you really understand what it means. I was impressed with her truthfulness and thanked her for being honest. There's no shame in wanting to know more to make educated financial decisions and certainly no shame in admitting where your gaps are. There are misunderstandings everywhere, fuelled by people not double-checking their assumptions.

The good news is you only have to understand one thing—your financial situation. If you don't own real estate, don't worry about real estate prices. If you don't own oil stocks, don't fret about dropping oil prices. Try, for your own peace of mind, to contain your anxieties to the specific situations that affect you and your life.

Of course I hope you still take an interest in the world around you for the benefit of others, but that is different from wearing a worried economic lens every time you pick up the newspaper. It may be that your first foray into financial empowerment is to start ignoring pieces of information and data that have no impact on you directly.

Education is at the heart of our mission at Sophia. We provide hundreds of people with free seminars and workshops over the course of a year, because we believe so strongly that so much pain and fear and poverty can be allayed if people have high-quality information. And yes, you only need to know what affects you personally, but that could still mean a lot of information. If you own an RRSP but don't understand either the structure or the holdings within it, then we can increase your effectiveness and lower your stress by pumping some knowledge into your brain. At first, learning hurts a bit. It is stretching you, your synapses are super-firing, and sometimes I see people reacting emotionally to this process. But this is temporary, like having sore muscles after your first workout following a long absence from the gym. It is for the greater good, but there may be a little kickback while you are getting started.

There was some fascinating research done a few years ago that showed how women are affected by knowledge. As they learn, they get braver and more able to take on risk, which is significant because assessing and managing risk is a huge component in creating and preserving wealth. With new knowledge comes increased capability. Increased capability leads to increased capacity, and that is worth the effort of expending time and resources.

The other part of knowing is related to emotional management. When you feel secure that you have all the information you need to make an informed decision, you will feel greater peace of mind. And as we discussed, peace of mind is a key component of balanced and more rational decision-making. So, read more books, attend workshops and seminars from reputable sources of financial literacy. These are major steps you can take to increase your wealth.

What do women really want to know about money?

There is a very big difference between talking about what a woman *needs* to know or *should* know about money and what she *wants* to know. In working with thousands of women about money, they all want to know in some way or another "Will I have enough?" and "How can I get the job done with the least amount of energy and involvement?" Women feel enormous time constraints. They say they're being pulled in so many different directions, and the reason they're not stepping up to the financial plate is that they don't have the time. This is often one area where the men in their life offer to help. It seems there's so little help given in other areas that financial management is at least one thing they can delegate without conflict.

Women also want to know how to get this all done without freaking out, losing sleep and antagonizing their husbands. It's a big worry.

Some questions that live in the hearts of women don't get asked but are thought about, and some get asked that are clever disguises for the real questions that lurk in their souls. That root question is often some kind of shadow or negative belief passed on from family or culture.

I also think there are some other things we should ask about that we probably haven't thought of yet, like what kind of insurance to get, what is power of attorney and how to manage capital gains (and maybe even, what is a capital gain). Maybe we want to know about the asset allocation structure in our RRSP but don't have the words to ask. Maybe we don't even know how much our RRSP is worth or even how much our spouse has in theirs. And maybe we might want to ask how much our husband is taking out of his RIF, and is the money going to last for our longer life expectancy if he keeps taking it out at this rate? And then the biggest question of all: What happens if we ask these questions?

We hear that people want security, a new car, a vacation in France, to not run out of money before they die, to be able to support their mom who is ill or their child who has special needs. We hear that people want to make money and not lose money. We hear that they want to understand what they are doing, or they want us to do it all for them and not talk about it. The questions we get are as far reaching as "How do I not lose money?" to "When will I have enough?" to "How can I make sure my kids can handle the money I leave them in the will?"

At the root of it all, we all want to know how to reconcile our values, love and relationships with money and power. We want to know how to be who we really are and use money to express that knowledge, to be authentic and not in conflict. Essentially, we want to use our power for the greater good while still being authentic and true to who we are.

The first thing I ask when I teach a workshop at our Sophia offices is either "What questions live in you?" or "What brings you here?" After doing hundreds of financial workshops, I simply open the questions up to the floor and I ask some version of "What do you want to know today that if you learn it, will make you feel like this morning has been well spent?" At first there is usually a heavy pause, and then the questions pour out. "Why am I in conflict about this?" "What is it that I *need* to know?" "How can I make sure I have enough?" "How can I make sure what I'm doing is working?"

Somehow we've been made to feel that our questions are stupid unless we articulate them perfectly. Women are extremely reluctant to ask these questions. If a woman doesn't understand her statements or plan or portfolio, I give her some language for her questions and then ask her to go back to her advisor and request for it to be explained differently. They say "Won't that make them think I'm stupid?" No, this is how powerful people talk to each other. They don't pretend to know things they don't understand, and they demand understanding. Your advisors are there to serve *you*, and you have a right to understand what you're being told. The saying "There are no stupid questions" has some merit but is not exactly accurate. It should be "All questions deserve answers." Some may not be very advanced. So what? They're our questions.

In a large workshop, it is common for a multi-millionaire to be sitting next to a woman in poverty. They have different lives and reasons for being there, but their questions can sound the same. That's why I can say with authority that someone with $3 million dollars can have the same anxiety level about her money as someone who's in debt $60,000. What they want to know is what they *need* to know. What the basic, elemental truths are. What the essential skills are. The knowledge that is absolutely necessary to not become a "bag lady."

A woman also wants to know what to do when people ask her questions she doesn't know how to answer. All these things are about negotiating or understanding who we really are economically and the role finances play in our lives.

MONEY BEHAVIOUR

This is the third component of our relationship with money: our behaviour, how we act. You can be the most knowledgeable person on the planet; you can read hundreds of books on the economy and portfolio optimization; you can have a strong belief system rooted in peace and prosperity; but if you never act on these strengths, it just doesn't matter. I see women every day who are locked into the endless pursuit of information or who continue to do affirmations while spending money they don't have on private Pilates classes. We have talked about some of the complexities of the psychology of money and touched on the role of knowledge, but we have to act.

So, where do we start? As usual, the inner journey is embarked on before an authentic, effective, external experience can manifest. The first internal questions sound like: Who am I? What are my values? What's my mission? What are my ideas? How will I get this to work out? What is money to me? What was money to my family? Those questions are the foundation of self-determination, have such weight behind them and are ready to have the light shone on them and be answered.

One thing I have learned about people and their money is that it is a dynamic, ever-changing journey, where there can be deep conflict. I try to help people locate their financial and personal pain points and collaborate on finding solutions that will alleviate the distress. Money hurts a lot of people.

When I was doing my doctoral work as a child psychologist, I worked at a preschool/research facility with three-to-four-year-olds. All the parents at one time or another came to me (and some several times) with versions of the same question: "Is my child weirder than all the others?" They want to know how their kids compare, how they measure up against the group.

This same question is commonly found at the centre of financial confusion and reflects the same anxieties: "Is my money doing the same kinds of things other people's money is?" Or a similar concern: "Am I more or less financially screwed up than other people?"

Last week, I talked to a woman who didn't think she had enough for food this week. Her kids were out selling lemonade on the corner to try to make money. Unfortunately, I don't think handing her money would solve the deeper problem. It had to do with her thought and behaviour processes. Her deep beliefs of scarcity and longing for the easy way out were creating tremendous tension. I wanted her to see the things as they are, without judgment, and systematically plan for a different outcome.

But none of this process can go forward if we don't operate from self-compassion. I have little judgment for anyone about these things, because the truth is the truth. We can tell the truth and be nice to ourselves while we do it, whether we're a millionaire or on welfare. And no, it's not easier if you're rich.

There are two realms that we concern ourselves with: the controllable and the uncontrollable. The global economy and taxes are uncontrollable. What's in our controllable realm? Our income, our expenses, our spending and where we live.

In the west side of Vancouver there are women who are eating beans and rice to save money, while sitting on $6 million

properties they don't want to leave because they are so committed to staying in the family home after a divorce. Their action is
driven by the widely held belief that children "need" to remain
in their original house. That's just not true. Children need to live
in a conflict-free environment. Whether that's a one-bedroom
condo or a 60-room mansion is of little consequence to a child.

Our attitude and impulses are also controllable. We have
the power to change our perspective. As we discussed earlier,
resentment and anger cloud our judgment and impede our
ability to make sound decisions. The more peaceful we are, the
cleaner the information is that we allow into our brains and the
better decisions we can make.

When unacknowledged needs and problematic thought
patterns are in control of our behaviour, it comes across in our
choices. We see this with compensatory and compulsory shopping habits, collecting shoes or other types of clothing or acces-
sories. Grounding ourselves in what's true and real for us helps
protect us from short-term reactionary decisions.

Doing what is right and good for us requires an alignment of
all the aforementioned principles. Right action is based on right
thinking and feeling. But you don't need to feel 100 per cent certain about every step before you take it. I am of the mind that
you can never be completely sure of any action you take. So, if
you're always waiting for that magical moment to arrive, you
may never do anything. And that in itself is a behaviour that
has just as many consequences as making a wrong decision. So,
you must do something. Interview new advisors, go to the bank,
read this book, create a cash flow statement or start a program
of positive self-talk. Take that first baby step, act on what you do
know and begin.

MONEY THROUGH
THE GENDER LENS

///////////////////////

I **HAVE BEEN** teaching various forms of a "women and investing" workshop since my first year as a financial advisor in the U.S. By now, I estimate that I have taught, on both sides of the border, about 4,000 women, and things tend to unfold in a pretty consistent manner.

Even though the women have registered and shown up for the investing workshop, they are still a bit skeptical. There is usually nervousness in the air. Some may even have a bit of a chip on their shoulder. They sit quietly, arms folded, shoulders tense. Sometimes they begin conversations and a kind of nervous group chatter ensues. I discern an unspoken apprehension, as though they are thinking, "Are you going to put us down too, because we're women?" or "Are you going to make me feel worse than I already do?"

They're not really sure whether the gender lens is going to benefit them or belittle them, so the first thing I do after introducing myself is throw the question out to the floor: "Why do *you* think I've brought only women here today?"

The answers are as varied as the women who offer them. They say, "Is it because we have babies?" "Because we aren't raised by our mothers to handle money?" "Is it that we don't know as much as men about money?" And they tell me, "If men were here they would not let us get a word in edgewise. They would dominate the conversation."

Some of the answers are quite surprising. Some I hear at every workshop, and some are a window into a particular woman's life at a particular time. But by the time we are through this sharing, they have provided me with the gender lens that is relevant for them. We have exposed the issues that need to be addressed and the questions that need to be answered that morning and we go from there.

The issue of gender and money evokes a wide range of reactions. For some, the whole subject feels smothering, a fog that can be so palpable and thick that people feel the weight of inertia dragging them down as they try to move through it. Women often just raise their hands in defeat. It's just too much, too prevalent, too hurtful, and we're too tired. When men hear us talk about these differences, they often get irritated: "What do they want anyway?" or defensive: "I would never put a woman down. I'm a good guy."

But the subtleties of sexism are often hard to find words for. One reason is that many of these beliefs exist deeply within us and often are entirely unconscious. There are sincere attempts to deal with and include women in the financial discussion, but unfortunately these are offset by the insincere messages. Women tell me they get a sense that they are being "bought off" with empty gestures of inclusion like having mutual funds prospectuses printed in pink ink, or by putting women in brochure pictures but still using charts and graphs and masculine language, or creating yet another women's task force to study the issue. There are so many shades of gender that infuse our culture. And many are almost invisible. We just know that we feel comfortable or we don't, feel included or not, with a place or language or person.

At Sophia, we hired a professional interior designer and took considerable time and effort to make sure our office décor communicated: "You are welcome here." It had to radiate warmth and hospitality while projecting the kind of seriousness that is associated with financial responsibility. It isn't about painting the walls pink or in any way saying, "Hey little girls, this place is for you to get smarter because we know you're so different." As women, we hate that. We hate it so much that we avoid any institution or business that approaches us like that. We often can't quite identify why we're so annoyed or disconnected, or why we feel so comfortable somewhere else. It's an invisible, sometimes ethereal communication of respect and inclusion that speaks directly to our hearts.

Two weeks ago, I attended a financial conference, and on my way into the networking opening reception I was greeted by young women dressed as Las Vegas showgirls, in skimpy outfits and high heels. To top it off, the organizers had set up photo podiums so that the men (average age 50) could have their pictures taken beside these half-dressed women young enough to be their daughters. Did the organizers actually think this was appropriate? Did they stop to consider how the few women participants would view this? These actions are subtle *and* outrageous *and* incessant. We can end up feeling diminished, degraded and dismissed, or we can put ourselves in environments where we feel uplifted, nourished and supported. I choose to do what it takes to experience the latter.

SEXISM AND SENSITIVITIES

I want to state clearly that I know that when gender is used as a filter for large and sweeping generalizations it can raise hackles. It can also be a subtle way of supporting prejudice (sexism) and can be very annoying and, frankly, quite discriminatory. The longer I work in this business, the more I have noticed how our sensitivity and prickliness gets intensified over time.

I have some ideas about this I will share later, and I hope to minimize these reactions. I will use observations, true stories and as much research as I can get in without boring you silly and creating angst in our legal compliance department. But I am just not prepared to leave gender issues off the table. Sometimes I feel like I am being bullied, that these issues are indeed the sacred cow of our society and there is increasing pushback when they are brought up.

I was asked to speak to a group of lawyers this year about gender and finance. They called me the week I was to present to say they felt my topic would be "inflammatory." I first asked what was inflammatory about delivering empirical data about the challenges they face every day in their professional careers. They said they feared it would create a rift within their group of lawyers, which was half male and half female. I said "If it's that difficult, don't you think it's something that should be put on the table and talked about?" On reflection, I am still not sure which was causing the angst—gender or finance. I have learned one really critical lesson in all this, and it can be summed up in the words of Robert Frost: "The best way out is always through." I'm not sure anymore that standing on the outside of burning issues serves anyone.

My worry is that if we don't look at and talk about gender issues, we will have a hard time finding our place on this journey of empowerment. There are things that I can control and things I can't. There are concerns that are mine alone and are part of my own psychological, physical and spiritual quest. There are concerns that I share with millions of others. And there are circumstances and issues that are clearly so unchangeable that my role is to simply notice them. Either way, I need them revealed so that I can decide how to navigate my way through. I have come to believe that without the airing of gender differences, we run a high risk of staying unconscious.

EVERY WOMAN is unique. She has her own personality, character, moral sense and emotional predilections. Each one of us is a product of our family of origin and from a different time and place. But as a gender group, there is much that we share.

There are genuine differences in the way men and women view and operate in the world. These gender distinctions are supported by a significant body of empirical data and can be summarized into four major areas where I've noticed that gender plays a significant part in how we approach money: We think differently than men do about money, communicate differently about it, are raised and conditioned differently, and are subject to different life circumstances.

LIFE CIRCUMSTANCES

There are three primary ways in which men and women's circumstantial differences can have significant economic impact. We earn less than men, we bear the children and we live longer.

Women's wages

As I dig into my files to look at the various research studies on the wage gap between men and women, there are several disparities. The gender wage-gap numbers for the U.S. and Canada come in anywhere from 20 cents on the dollar to up to 38 cents, depending on how the calculations are done and who has done them. I am not sure the actual number even matters at this point. The fact is that there is a gap, women earn less, and there are many factors affecting it.

Most women will choose to or need to leave and re-enter the workforce at some point in their lives to meet family caregiving responsibilities. We tend to congregate in traditionally undervalued and low-paying jobs, such as child care and clerical work. We seek out work environments that have flexibility and part-time employment. Often these are smaller employers, and these kinds of jobs tend to have lower wages. There is also less unionization among female workers. Interestingly, discrimination in hiring, promotion and compensation practices in the workplace is usually assessed as being only about 10 to 15 per cent of the wage gap. The remaining issues are ones that we control.

A recent study showed the average female physician in British Columbia bills 50 cents for every dollar a male physician bills. It's not a result of wage discrimination, because the government has standard rates for set tasks. It goes deeper than that. Women spend more time with their patients, they are less likely to specialize and they are less likely to own their own practise or medical building. These are a set of choices coming out of thinking about other people, our families and our values, but they have some insidious and significant consequences. It's not that we want to undervalue ourselves—it's a series of micro-assumptions and small decisions that ultimately adds up to a significant financial disadvantage.

Child rearing

Being the child bearers is simply a biological capability, and giving birth to children is not in itself enough to cause financial issues. It is our behaviour, choices and assumptions after children are born that have the huge impact. A recent paper called *Career Interrupted: The Economic Impact of Motherhood* put out by TD in 2010 goes into some depth looking at the complex array of consequences that motherhood has for women.

Male managers are often heard referring to parental leave as "taking time off from work," which is a discriminatory attitude and incorrect. This "time off" leads to us working in lesser positions when we do come back to work, losing money in our pensions and retirement savings, needing to get re-credentialed, missing opportunities and having to work more hours to "prove" ourselves.

A woman friend of mine from one of Canada's top accounting firms consciously timed her pregnancy and parental leave to fall between two tax seasons. On her return to work after six months leave, she was still penalized by her firm by docking her a year towards partnership. The reason given was that she "took time off," and "it wasn't fair to her male colleagues who had stayed and worked" if she was treated differently. Her male colleagues advanced ahead of her. She was furious and began planning her exit strategy. She left a year later and never mentioned that it was this discrimination that led to her decision. I worry that this continues to reinforce the masculine paradigm that mothers are unreliable workers.

I recently had a discussion with a high-ranking member of the RCMP who also said that although women have what it takes to be great officers, they just don't take the job seriously after they have kids—that "they have competing roles." I suggested that maybe there were other issues at play and told him several stories I had heard directly from women. I proposed that maybe women sometimes just used the excuse that they had family responsibilities because it was socially acceptable. Maybe, for some of these women, it was frustration over ongoing harassment or the constant barrage of subtle and incessant sexist behaviours that led to their departure. I told him the story of the showgirls at the conference and how upsetting I found it. That my stomach had been in knots and I felt so put down and out of place. He listened, but I could see that it was an overwhelming concept for him to even contemplate.

If it is true that we sometimes use motherhood as a shield, then we do a great disservice to the other women behind us by not standing up and actually talking about the real issues behind our behaviour and, ultimately, our departures. I must also say I am sympathetic and understand that most women I know who have worked hard for their professional accreditation do not want to "burn bridges."

There are of course very real pressures and conflicts that arise from motherhood. The deep desire to be the best mother we can be while advancing our career can be a minefield of stress and competing responsibilities. Child care issues, inflexible work hours and duties, transit issues, illness and special needs of children can all interfere with work. And these are generally viewed and accepted as a woman's issue. Rarely have I seen men express dissatisfaction with balancing fatherhood and work. Add to that the wiring we have for connection and nurturing and we have a mess of circumstances that can interfere with our careers and peace of mind. It can get very complicated, and I am so glad this area is not my primary focus—it's the economic repercussions that interest me. And for once, that is the easier area of challenge to overcome.

The inherent financial conflict is that motherhood is very highly valued emotionally, somewhat valued socially but of no real value economically, other than to be detrimental. When a mother chooses to stay at home to raise children, there are other financial implications that have a far-reaching impact.

This period of non–wage earning is often the point when women relinquish control of family finances. Women say that child rearing is exhausting and they are too tired and often too overwhelmed to balance the cheque book and study the RRSP statements. But I believe it goes a bit deeper. I think we are often happy to have that burden lifted. Financial responsibility is a weighty load.

In addition, I hear women say that they actually don't feel that the household income is their money anymore. In the dark chambers of many women's psyche lurks the belief that child care is not a financially equivalent role. They think they aren't "earning" money, so they do not have the right to weigh in on the larger financial matters or even to give input. It is also during these years that a man's retirement benefits gain momentum. This is when women will look to their partners to take over the bulk of the wage-earning responsibilities, and with that money comes power. It can affect what expenditures are made, what kind of housing is purchased and even the geographic location of the family. I have watched women repeatedly shrug their shoulders in defeat. He earns the money. He makes those decisions. And I will also tell you it's a rare modern woman who will admit this either to herself or her friends.

Lifespan

The third circumstance is longevity. The statistic that inspired so much research and activity at Smith Barney in the late '90s was that if a woman hits the age of 50 without a life-threatening illness, her life expectancy is 94. Just this morning, I went online to do a life expectancy calculator, and indeed, even with both my parents having died in their sixties, I still came out at 94.8 years.

The idea of an increasing lifespan has several high-impact repercussions. I have met with women in their mid-eighties who will be out of money in a couple of years, or even a few months. They all say to me, with varying degrees of panic, "I never expected to live this long!" They are worried sick about what to do for the rest of their lives. Financial plans are rarely projected out into the mid-nineties for women.

The matching of financial resources to life expectancy is one of the most difficult tasks in money management. The biggest factor is that none of us knows when we will die. If you die next week, you probably have enough to be retired comfortably. If it happens in 55 years, you might be stretched quite thin. But as you'd imagine, running out of money is what we want to avoid, because even if you die one week after you run out, it makes for a very bad week.

The old precept that money had to be "safe" and conservatively managed to provide for retirement was based on realties that no longer exist. In 1960, the year I was born, the average adult white male worker died 2.7 years after he retired. Of course, you can put your money in bonds or cash if you only have to live off your savings for two or three years. Many people now have retirements that can last forty years! This is a huge shock to any financial plan (not to mention the nervous system) when you look at it closely.

In conclusion, if you put lower lifetime wages with an extended absence from the workforce and subsequently lower pensions, and add that to longer life expectancies, we have a recipe for poverty soup! And this is without even talking about the sharp increase in the number of divorces for people who have been in marriages for 25 years or more. We cannot ignore the new realities facing us as women. Our financial survival depends on it.

CONDITIONING

In the socio-cultural realm, our behaviour is placed in the context of our society and the cultural values that shape us. One of the key challenges in having the discussion about these influences is their invisibility. At a week-long conflict resolution course I attended, they often used the phrase "the air we breathe, the water we swim in" to describe this phenomenon. It so clearly expresses the difficulty we have in being awake to our own biases and assumptions.

The expectations of those around us are felt keenly and shape our experiences profoundly, but we are often unaware of them. We just "go with the flow" most of the time. Sometimes we see what is happening and decide it's just not worth the trouble to address it, but most often these expectations are simply not recognized or examined.

I ask the participants in my classes about how they think women and men are different in the ways they experience the world with regard to finances. The answers are diverse, but the most common one is "Women don't know as much about money as men." I press further with "What does that mean?"

They often respond that they were never taught about money at home and wonder why they were never taught about the financial part of life in school.

We dig deeper, and I point out that the lack of personal finance in families or in the school curriculums should result in men not knowing about money too, but they've just claimed men know more. I explain the research that says men consistently overestimate their financial knowledge and women underestimate theirs. And now we get into the heart of the matter. Regardless of what is real, both genders seem to believe that it's the man's "job" to understand and manage the finances, while many women seem to feel it is someone else's responsibility to teach them how to do it.

I want to clarify here that when I talk about household finances, I am not talking about the grocery budget or balancing the cheque book. The general consensus in business literature is that women make about 80 per cent of the household buying decisions, and the lion's share of the daily dollar management falls on their shoulders, like the other menial home-making tasks. I'm talking about the "big money": the stocks, bonds, RRSPs and commercial property. I'm talking about understanding leverage and mortgages.

We have already discussed many of these issues in previous chapters. Women seem to have a deep-seated belief that caring for others and being cared for is fundamental to our identity and self-worth. And maybe it is. But the repercussions of this on our relationship to money are huge.

Another area where I see how women and men value different qualities is in the area of appearance. We make comments about each other's clothing, shoes and new haircuts. Yesterday, a professional told me how nice my skin looked! (I was flattered and later quite pleased with this confirmation that my new skin product line must be working.) Frankly, it was the most memorable aspect of our meeting. What does that say? This is a social habit that is intended to create rapport, and it does. But I have never seen a man walk up to another one, shake his hand and cry out, "Jim, I love the hair!" Take a look at what you think the underlying value assumptions are.

There is great pressure on us to be loving mothers, good cooks and still be CEO of a multinational corporation. And preferably, as CEO, we should earn well but less than our husbands—or at least pretend to socially so we don't embarrass them. But none of this is ever really talked about. Why should my income have anything to do with my husband's self-esteem and vice versa? Begin to answer that question and you open the sociocultural Pandora's box.

I gave a talk at a leadership conference where a participant told the group how she had set up her own cash flow and banking systems. She was very proud of the financial steps she was taking, and she should be. Then she made a comment that she hadn't really had to worry about financial planning before because her former partner earned so much that money wasn't a problem. I waited for the group to catch that statement. I waited, and they watched me waiting, but they didn't even flicker. I then asked her why being or not being in a relationship had any bearing on whether she took responsibility for her finances. The room was still stumped. That is what I mean about invisible cultural assumptions that run deep within us.

There is a quote I ponder sometimes: "When money is plenty, it is a man's world. When money is scarce, it is a woman's world." It was taken from the *Ladies' Home Journal* October 1932 edition. Is this a compliment to our resourcefulness, ingenuity and strength? Is that when we move into high gear? When the going gets tough...blah blah blah? Or is it a recognition that we operate comfortably only in the world of scarcity or when there aren't many dollars to manage? I wish I could make sense of it.

Should I tell you the stories of how women pretend in their relationships so that they won't rock the boat? I know a brilliant woman realtor, acknowledged for her professional acumen and success, who "allowed" her husband, a roofing contractor, to negotiate the sale of their home. She didn't want him to feel inferior. Or the gifted feminist scientist whose husband "won't let her see" RRSP statements, and she doesn't want to upset him by pushing the issue. Or the partner at a large accounting firm whose husband, a teacher, manages their RRSPS and even has discretionary authority over their accounts. You know what I'm talking about and have seen it over and over. What is that story about? This kind of play-acting appears to "keep the peace," but we are left to wonder, at what cost? What is the belief system that fuels these behaviours?

If you go to a cocktail party, you can hear men talking sports, business, the stock market and the economy. In my first years as a broker, I would try to join in; I loved those topics, as you can imagine. I began to notice that my contributions were met with consternation. The men often felt a need to let me know that, regardless of my professional education, they could teach me a few things. And when I tried to bring up these subjects when talking to women, they looked at me like I'd grown a second head (had I?) and efficiently moved the conversation back to one of their interests. Eventually, I learned that if I wanted to have any social contact, I needed to revert to more traditional topics of conversation.

Clearly, awareness is critical to empowerment. We need to recognize the forces around us and put some thought towards their effect on our feelings and behaviour. Maybe you could start to stir things up in areas where you are comfortable. Talk about money at the dinner table with your kids. Share first-pay-cheque stories or what you read in the news on the first page of the business section today. Awaken to how the things you say may be interpreted by young ears. Try to move a discussion now and again at a dinner party to some of the things you've been reading about money or what your banker said about opening a TFSA. You don't even have to know what you are really talking about. Model curiosity. You can gracefully challenge stereotypes by behaving in a different away and see what happens.

Charlotte Perkins Gilman wrote a book called *Women and Economics: A Study of the Economic Relation Between Men and Women as a Factor in Social Revolution.* In it, she says that humans are the only species where the female is dependent on the male for survival and that this dependence requires that women pay off their debt through domestic services or "sex-functions." The result is that the women "work longer and harder than most men, and not solely in maternal duties." She argues that these sexual distinctions have led to an odd distribution of power and are detrimental to both genders, and that these sexual distinctions leave women behind and have allowed men to claim credit for human progress. She says that women fulfill the dual roles of "mother" and "martyr" and pass these roles down to their children, creating a continuing image of women as unpaid workers and nurturers. This in turn has stunted women's creative and personal growth.

After I read these passages to my classes, I ask whether this resonates with them. "Oh, yes!" is the consistent reply. Her book was published in 1898.

THOUGHT PROCESSES

Most women would agree that we think differently from men, and most scientists concur. But this can be a touchy subject for some. The tendency is to either make sweeping generalizations or, conversely, to want to completely ignore the differences.

If we acknowledge that we are different, the presupposition is that someone is going to be proven to be inferior. In fact, the more research I do and the more I see examples of decision-making by both genders, the more convinced I am of their complementary nature and that, ideally, we should be making decisions together.

One interesting area of brain research has looked at the function and gender differences of the portion of the brain called the corpus collosum. This wide, flat bundle of neural fibers lies deep in the centre of the brain and is the juncture, or bridge, between the left and right hemispheres, facilitating communication between the two sides of the brain. Simply put, the left hemisphere handles the cognitive, rational functions, while the right hemisphere handles emotion and creative functions. Although there is some debate, the prevailing thought is that women have more of these neural fibers in a larger collosum, which means they can transfer data faster between the two sides of the brain, allowing for rational thought and emotion to communicate more efficiently, giving rise to balanced and relative thinking.

With more neural connections linking the left and right brains, women are wired to work more comfortably with facts and emotions simultaneously and with greater ease than most men. Men tend to switch functions with greater effort. So, if women are wired to have both parts of the brain talk more efficiently to each other, they can be both creative and logical simultaneously. We think holistically and contextually. We are wired to think about implications and consequences.

I am often heard to say that a woman can be crying and balancing a cheque book at the same time. A useful skill in some families. Men generally can't do this as easily. They have to cry, stop crying and then do the math.

When women want to talk to men, they tend to cue them with a particular phrase: "Honey, we need to talk." That is a signal for the man to move from his logical brain into the feeling side of his brain, because he's about to have an emotional conversation. Women tend to move easily between concrete and abstract, data and emotion. We easily apply meaning to the dollars.

Because we think more holistically, it's essential for a woman to have a personal, meaningful financial plan that has emotional and social context. The charts, graphs and numbers come afterward. I had one woman tell me she was put on earth to save birds—a particular species in a specific state—and that became part of her financial framework. It was fundamental to how she thought about herself and money. When a woman talks about money, she will typically talk about it as a means to an end, not an end itself. This makes sense in terms of our neurology.

Scientific evidence suggests that hormonal factors influence formation of various brain structures in males and females, and this hard-wires us to process information differently.

Dr. Joan Meyers-Levy is one of my best resources when it comes to summarizing neurological differences between the male and female brains. After decades of gender research, she has postulated the "selectivity hypothesis." Men "eliminate" data and women "integrate" data when they process information. Men focus on a few cues and often use simple decision-making rules, such as a salesperson's recommendation or speed. Men tend to focus on objective claims and have a kind of stripped-down processing that is often fast and efficient. Women, however, consider more angles and use more sources of information when they make decisions. They try to get all the information possible before they decide on something. In Meyers-Levy's words, "Women notice absolutely everything." She also says that females generally attempt to engage in "an effortful, comprehensive, piecemeal analysis of all available information."

The downside of women having more thorough decision-making processes is that we take so much longer to make a decision. Women will examine all possible scenarios that might affect the decision and are often afraid of making a mistake. I have called this tendency the Fuss Factor.

When women are making decisions in areas where they do not feel confident, we will often attempt to collect information from everywhere and everyone. There doesn't seem to be a rationale behind the selection of the sources. We will trust our psychologist as much as our next-door neighbour, as much as the mail carrier. Then we either become inert or delve into levels of detail that obscure the common sense solution that may be staring us in the face. The fussing isn't only a laborious process, it also leads us to focus on micro-elements that have little to do with the overall issue.

When my women-only gym recently closed, I was quite curious about the way the members went about deciding on their next step in choosing another facility. One woman became obsessed with the parking garage security, another with the size of the washroom. Instead of looking at the Big Picture, which we are wired to do naturally, we circumvent our own processes and move to the dark side of obsessive details, which essentially paralyzes us. It is the shadow side of one of our best cognitive advantages and can lead to very time-consuming, effortful decision-making.

This plays into our concern that managing money is time consuming and that we don't have time for it. If it takes us five times longer than a man to make a decision, and we are already time-strapped, then of course it's daunting. Our own decision-making processes need to be addressed and efficiencies developed so that it does not take so much time. Right now, for many, it's a lose-lose proposition.

How we think affects our approach to risk

There is a great deal of examination of the issue of women, men and risk-taking, and equally as much controversy around it. German scientists conducted an experiment on a virtual BMX track. After the physiological testing, the men responded "Wooh! That was great! Let's do it again!" When women finished the sequence, they reported that they hated it and felt sick to their stomachs. The researchers proposed that there are innate physiological differences that affect our approach and response to volatility and risk.

In 2002, in an important study conducted by Gysler, Kruse and Schubert, women were shown to be significantly more risk-averse, with their risk aversion decreasing significantly with increased knowledge. The interactions have just the opposite effect for men, whose risk aversion *increases* the more information they receive. Think about the implications of that!

A commonly held perception is that men seem to take more risks, whereas women tend to be more conservative. I often say that an intelligent woman facing a lack of knowledge reverts to conservatism. Understanding and risk management are highly correlated for women investors in that the more they know, the more risk they are prepared to take on. The average woman wants to fully understand what is going on and the consequences of her decisions before she commits to them. She needs to feel confident and informed. Men are most able to take risks when they have minimal information about the downside consequence of a decision.

The whole investing world is built on fast appointments and rapid transactions, the masculine model it often favours. Meetings with a traditional stockbroker are set up to be finished within twenty minutes. I have seen this at both of the firms I worked for. In that male construct, fast processes create more confident, decisive male investors—but it's the exact opposite of what women need!

Even when the Fuss Factor has not been activated, women tend to take two to three times longer than men to make financial decisions. The upside to this is that in the best case scenario those decisions are well informed. It takes time to fully understand a problem and the consequences of potential solutions. The downside, of course, is the extra expenditure of a woman's most precious resource: time.

In an article published in *Psychology Today* in 2003, Hara Estroff Marano found that women seem to be hard-wired for a top-down, big-picture view. Men are wired to look at things from the bottom up (no surprise there). Men focus first on minute detail, and operate most easily with a certain detachment. Women tend to focus on the environment around that subject and its relative context. It's not that women can't understand the charts and graphs that men love, it's that it's all irrelevant until context is established.

This plays out in the financial world on a daily basis. When a woman comes into my office and I ask her, "What brings you here?" she begins a thorough and comprehensive overview of the important people and situations in her life, what she is worried about and what she needs money to do. Men most often pull out their investment statements and begin pointing to specific holdings, or they talk about one thing that has really made them angry.

One neurological predisposition is not better than the other. There are positives and negatives to seeing the big and small picture, and both approaches are useful in different contexts. In the world of money, processing consequences, looking at the full picture, then taking definitive action is a great skill. Money is not a separate entity from your life, and you lose some of its power when this is forgotten. But if the details stress you out so much that you are forced into inertia, then that is not good either.

LANGUAGE

The world's leading psycholinguist, Deborah Tannen, author of more than ten books on men and women's conversational styles, has much to say about how we communicate. She explains that women communicate in order to create relationships, facilitate interaction and exchange feelings. We speak and hear a language of connection and intimacy. We affiliate. Men, however, speak in hierarchal forms, which she summarizes as "report talk" versus women's "rapport talk."

Dr. Judy Rosener also posits that men speak and hear a language of status and independence. They communicate to obtain information, establish their status and demonstrate independence. These significant differences in language are experienced daily at work, at home and most definitely in the world of money. A good example of this is that women often nod through an entire workshop with me. For women, nodding in this way does not mean agreement. It's a social cue to encourage me to continue speaking. I know that nodding means they are paying attention, following along and being "nice." A man, however, will interpret nodding as agreement. This one physical gesture can lead to a buildup of *assumed* answers and ideas that leads to miscommunication and conflict.

When I hear women say, "I don't know how I signed that document" or "My husband says he invested all the money from our house into a company," I imagine that as they were talking, she was nodding and listening, not consenting. He interpreted her pleasant demeanour and nods as acquiescence.

The problem with nodding in a financial discussion is that men may end up believing that we've agreed to their decisions, then act on them nearly immediately, and we are too nervous to challenge this assumption.

Women say they feel dominated by men in financial conversations, and I must say my experience aligns with that. I can't tell you how often men with no education or experience try to tell me about the stock market or world economics. I watched a male advisor at lunch last week tell a female advisor, who was also a branch manager with forty people reporting to her, how she should be investing her clients' money. I was stunned to watch her nod and smile for almost twenty straight minutes while this boor bored us nearly to death. Finally, I snapped and intervened because it looked like we could have been there forever.

When women come to my women-only workshops, they often say it is the first time they felt they could ask financial questions freely. Sometimes I playfully ask them what would happen if I let men in. They reply quickly that the men would take over and we'd all sit there quietly planning our grocery lists in our heads. That just about says it all.

Women also are more willing to express their lack of knowledge—sometimes too eagerly. They will go into a financial advisor's office and come right out and say they don't understand their statements or investments or will ask what to do next. This reflects a commendable willingness to learn and is most definitely not an issue of intelligence. It's because no one has ever explained the terms to them properly, in a language they can relate to.

Women regularly report that when they ask their male advisors to explain an issue or concept that they don't understand, the advisor will respond by repeating what he has just said verbatim but with a raised voice. The women then get uncomfortable. Instead of asking for different words or a different explanation, we back down. There's that need for affiliation again.

I often say that women are "branchy" and men are "trunky." Men tend to do things sequentially, using a confined, vertical process—their language reflects their directionality. Women like to process ideas out loud, moving through various scenarios verbally, all the while keeping track of their main idea. We use more words. We talk for longer lengths of time. And when we get excited, our voices go higher and speed up. All of these linguistic predilections are associated socio-culturally with a lack of power.

The long and short of it is that the willingness of women to be conciliatory in conversation can lead to a significant power imbalance when dealing with men. And that leads us into the area of conflict and negotiation.

Effective self-advocacy

I believe that negotiation is the most important skill in financial empowerment and the foundation of self-determination.

The first task is to define what truly matters to us as individuals. That's the basis of all financially empowered behaviours. Then we put our negotiation skills to use in speaking up for ourselves. You become a truly powerful investor when you are able to marry strategy to values.

Much of our experience in the world, in one way or another, is in interacting with men, who generally view and respond to conflict and negotiation very differently than we do as women. One factor in how we navigate differently is the limbic system of the brain, which governs emotion and response at a deep, intrinsic level. Current research has demonstrated that females on average have a larger, deeper limbic system, and this means that women are more in touch with and better able to express their feelings than men. This also means they have an increased need to bond and may actually *require* connection with others to experience optimal health and increase life expectancy. This helps explain our ability to communicate and express ourselves in relationships, but it also gives us some idea of why we have ended up so poorly equipped to handle the conflict and negotiation tasks that life throws at us.

In 2012, the engineering department at the University of British Columbia tracked the employment of their students five years after graduating and were appalled to discover that the women who graduated at the same time, in the same job market, in the same city, were making a third less than their young male counterparts. They looked into this and discovered that the female grads had one distinguishing commonality—none of them had questioned the salary they had been offered. This reluctance to negotiate starts young and has significant long-term financial consequences.

Women tend to see these situations in "yes or no" terms. Either we accept the job at the offered salary, or we don't get the job. Either we accept the marriage in its current state, or we won't have a marriage.

During a presentation I gave last summer, I brought up the necessity of asking for what we want. The minute we do ask, we set up a chain of events that can have a huge impact on our lives. As I was going down this path, I could feel the room start to tremble. Finally, a woman about 30 years old stood up and said, "But if I talk to my husband about wanting to run some of the money, he'll leave me." I asked why she thought this and how many other women in the room felt the same way, and most of them nodded their heads.

Then I asked them, "If you try to negotiate your salary with your boss, do you think he's going to fire you?" I was shocked that the same women nodded their heads again. In these women's minds, there was enormous fear of catastrophe if they started to become empowered and ask for what they were worth. This fear is largely irrational. People don't get fired for asking for a raise, and marriages don't implode if you ask to talk about your RRSP. If there are other unresolved issues underlying these conversations, then yes, you may be opening Pandora's box. But allowing the issues of power, control and poor communication to remain unacknowledged doesn't protect you from them. They are still hurting you. It's just not visible yet.

In the employment world, we are forced to face up to our predisposition towards connection and its "sister," conflict avoidance. When you don't negotiate an employment offer, you're almost always leaving money on the table, meaning you end up essentially subsidizing the next employee who does negotiate. Women tend to want to be liked and are often so happy at being approved of and accepted that they don't want to risk any form of rejection.

If an employer has already extended a job offer to you, they're not going to take it off the table just because you ask for more money. You may not get the money, but they're still going to be interested in you for the job.

In a job setting, it's helpful to understand that men treat negotiation like a sport. It's playtime. Women tend to imagine that the process will lead to some awful conclusion.

If we do take a stab at asking for a better offer, our own analysis of the experience often supports that flawed perception. If a woman asks for a $50,000 yearly salary instead of the $40,000 offered, and the employer counters with, "We're sorry, the best we can do is $42,000," there's a tendency for her to misinterpret the response as denial and rejection, which is a long way from a sport! Or the employer might use words to the effect of: "We really want you here, but times are tough, and we need team players here. We hope you can accept this lower offer." We're convinced that "taking one for the team" will work out in the long run, but it often doesn't.

Human resources' job is to get the best candidate (you) for as little money as possible. Your job is to get as much as possible without hurting that organization or being obnoxious.

Researching pay equity websites can give you the lay of the land regarding reasonable salary expectations and may boost your confidence.

Sometimes you may have to be prepared to walk away if a company really doesn't have enough to offer you for your services.

It's like dating, to some degree. "I really like you, but you're a smoker, and I'm having a hard time getting past that." "Well, I'm having trouble quitting smoking," they might say. Sometimes you just have to draw a line. "That's okay, just come back to me when you've been able to quit." Negotiation is just like that—reaching agreement through discussion and cooperation.

The truth is that *negotiation is a learnable skill* that combines personal style with some knowledge of how it works. Carrie Gallant, a negotiation specialist for women, says that when women are empowered with the skills and knowledge they need, they can negotiate results as good as or better than men's.

This fits with our understanding of our strong communication and emotional aptitude. Because women are inherently more adept at demonstrating their attentiveness (men have been proven to be just at good at listening as women, just not as good at showing it), empathizing and building relationships, they are more than adequately equipped to be powerful negotiators.

Many women find negotiating for their own wants and needs much more challenging than negotiating or advocating on behalf of others. In both cases, to be successful it is equally important to be able to influence others so that they will cooperate with you and to know when to say no and ask for something better.

One of the most significant impediments to this for women is the belief that asking for something more is rude or selfish, when, really, it is the pathway to self-respect and better relationships. When we change our personal "story" to reflect a broader picture of this practise, we are better able to take on the challenges of mastering it. Carrie is well known in our circles for telling women to be their own White Knight. No one else is going to go after the things that will make your life work for you as well as you. No one knows you as well as you, and frankly, no one is as invested in the outcome.

A common theme that comes up in meetings with women when they talk about handling money disagreements in their relationships is: "I don't want to rock the boat." Why are we so scared to speak up about something that affects us so much? I have heard women mentally track through the eventualities of domestic financial issues from the initial conflict straight through to divorce and the end of their families. With some women, there's a sense that a terrible calamity will result if they challenge the status quo.

It follows, then, that the most difficult negotiations happen at the kitchen table. I am again referring to discussions around motherhood, child care and leaving the workforce to care for children and not insisting on equal roles in child rearing and a fair and equitable distribution of housework. It makes sense that with our highly developed need for connection, this is where our negotiations are least effective and most challenging. We will do almost anything to maintain peace at home. We will sacrifice ourselves and our emotional well-being to keep our family together or not anger a spouse.

I could write a whole book on love, money and power that just deals with the issue of choosing connection and affiliation over personal financial well-being and autonomy. But we want to be able to handle not just our home life with a sense of personal power but the outside world as well. My wish is that every woman would be able to ask the bank manager for clarification on the role of her account manager, or to address a situation where she was treated poorly. I would like a woman to be comfortable asking for a change of doctor or a second opinion, a better price on a car or a break on her service fees. I would like to see women practise in low-stakes situations—like outside the home where relationships aren't on the line—and develop their own unique language of negotiation. For some, it may be about how to overcome nervousness or use sentences that are more conciliatory while being powerful. Each one of us has a different style, and it can be one of grace and poise, or fire and assertion. It's up to you.

Sometimes you need to be flexible in your interactions. I was recently asked to talk to an organization about strategic thinking. I declined because I didn't feel knowledgeable about that topic. They called back and said the women just really wanted to hear me talk, and it didn't really matter if I was knowledgeable on the subject or not.

I got there and asked the crowd, "What does a woman do if she is asked to come in to speak to a group of people about a subject she doesn't know about?" One reply was "You could bullshit your way through!"

I said, "Yes, you could. What are advantages and disadvantages of that?" An advantage would be that there's no need for prep time or to learn something new, but there's a disadvantage that's too large—when we are out of our depth, we "leak" our emotions. Sweat would start pouring, my face would show my nervousness and fear, and it would be obvious to the group that I was trying to fool them.

We talked for almost two hours about how to work together to create superior outcomes and as a group concluded that strategic thinking had a lot to do with being honest about yourself and the situation you find yourself in and using the power of open communication with others to find answers.

Negotiation and collaboration are not about faking it or trying to get something over on someone, so you can do what I did if you are put on the spot or out of you comfort zone. I just went with it and played my way though it, modeling authenticity while creating very dynamic discussion. That was a win-win outcome for everyone, including me, as I got to stretch myself.

I believe that the number one skill women need to learn to become truly financially empowered is negotiation. How many of us have to negotiate with someone or something to get somewhere? It happens every day, everywhere, all the time, with people in various relationships with us. It certainly should happen at a financial advisor's office. We need to learn to speak up and tell them if we're not following their charts and graphs, and if they need to use different terms.

I think women are too often taken advantage of in these situations. We forget we're paying these people for advice and there is more than one way to explain something. It's the advisor's responsibility to make sure their client understands everything and your duty to ensure that they do their job.

Women also need to learn negotiation young. When I am asked to teach at the high school level, I usually tell them that the last thing a teenage girl wants to learn about is something she thinks she won't need to know for ten years. The truth is, the developmentally appropriate task to teach in the teen years is negotiation. This is a fundamental skill set that affects all areas of a person's life, from agreeing on a rate for babysitting to saying, "No, I'm not going to have sex with you now, and this is why." It gives you the ability to stand up for yourself. If the energy of money is power, then the ability to direct it is in negotiation.

Last Christmas, my 15-year-old daughter was short-changed for a dog-sitting job for a neighbour. She knew that they were high payers for babysitting, so she was excited about looking after "Rover" for them. She had to significantly change her Christmas holidays to accommodate his care. But when she completed the job, she received an envelope of money that was about one-third of what she'd been expecting. Her first reaction was to say nothing, then once home, to sob uncontrollably. Then she got mad.

When she finally calmed down, I said to her, "What do you see as the options here?" After contemplating never babysitting again and several other extreme scenarios, she arrived at: "I could tell them I don't feel this is the right amount of money."

Over the next hour or so I talked to her about how she would negotiate this and even pointed out why she should have established her pricing up front. She finally got up her courage and emailed them, saying something like, "I know I should have discussed this prior to doing the work for you, and I really love working for you guys, and I like your dog, but because of how much you were paying for babysitting, I was expecting to get $15 per day for looking after Rover, and I only received $8. I don't mean to be rude, but..."

She received an email the next day from the mother saying, "Oh no, I can't believe you only got that amount, my husband must've made a mistake, of course we're going to give you the amount you want, we really appreciate your work too." So, not only did she get her usual daily rate, she got a guilt-tip. That's at the age of 15. I'm not too worried about her ability to negotiate for a salary later in life.

Women have a tendency to try to rescue other women from the fire instead of walking with them through it and helping them move forward along the journey. I could have jumped on the blaming bandwagon with my daughter to "help her feel better," but I didn't think that was the best solution, even though I was sad she was so upset. We can't keep avoiding the fire of our life tasks. And we can't just stand around saying, "Gosh it's so hot out here. Give me some lemonade!" We have to move through it. Then it cools down. Often we stand outside the heated situation and think, "I wonder how much worse it's going to be inside." But that's the big misunderstanding—it's much hotter in the ring outside the core. So, you might as well put on your fire gear and get on with moving through.

FINANCIAL
PLANNING

//////////////////////

FINANCIAL PLANNING is everything we've been discussing up until now in this book. We have been readying ourselves internally for the part of the journey that can really get us going—both emotionally and practically.

There are essentially five financial questions that inform the planning process. Each question leads to the next one. Every plan should have each of these questions addressed before an investment strategy even begins to be discussed! Have you noticed how few "shoulds" I've used up until now? That's because I don't like lecturing (well, maybe a bit) or being lectured (not at all). But this is one case where I just cannot see the sense in any other approach. Your investments serve your plan. Money serves the person. Not the other way around.

The five questions that inform the financial planning process are:

1. Where am I now?
2. Do I have cash reserve?
3. Where am I headed?
4. How do I get there?
5. How do I stay on track?

Together, these questions make up a systematic five-step process that can expand, contract and be adjusted to fit any time and circumstance of your life. Don't panic if you don't know the answers to them right now. I am going to lead you through the questions one by one and show you how to find your own answers.

Before financial planning can happen, it's very beneficial to have a grip on your emotions. This process does not inherently have judgment attached to it, unless you choose to place it there. You will apply your skills of observation, objectivity and self-awareness to keep you on the good path. If you do experience some emotional activation, you don't have to solve it—just notice it. If you feel any panic, self-loathing or shame come up, just forgive yourself and the emotion and keep moving forward. If there is a particular value or intention or life event that has brought you to this starting place, simply acknowledge it. The more emotionally intact you are entering this process, the easier it is.

We all need to learn how to make well-informed financial decisions and to understand the relationship between risk, asset allocation and rate of return, the structure of basic investment vehicles and the role of debt and surplus in wealth.

HOW DO I START?

From here. Right now.

Most of the women who I meet in my practise are forced to learn about money because of some large event that is happening in their life, such as divorce, widowhood, retirement or selling a business. Some women stay in the dark for a long time, then something hits them that makes them jump up, run to the window and open the curtains. The precipitating event can either be a joyful one or it can be sad. Regardless, when you're not accustomed to light in your eyes, it can hurt a bit at first. Or a lot.

Wanting to learn about money can also be precipitated by the recognition that our life won't go on forever, a kind of epiphany that the way things are can't be continued. It could be a realization that challenges the way you thought life was supposed to be. This can force someone to review the way they've acted so far, and that can be painful. But this self-awareness and the motivation to look inside ourselves is the first step of a journey that can shape a better, richer life.

Having been born and bred into money does have advantages. Certain assumptions and beliefs that are presumably functional get passed on to you. There is a wider margin of comfort. You are learning from a place where shelter and food are covered, or more. You may have learned important financial concepts sitting at the supper table and have a team of the city's top experts just waiting to hear from you. Just read Barbara Stanny's book *Prince Charming Isn't Coming: How Women Get Smart About Money* if you want to hear about the advantages and disadvantages of being born into wealth.

The big advantage to entering the learning curve when you are not starving or frantic is that you have some emotional and financial padding to buffer you and a safety net to catch you if you make mistakes. The hardest job in the world is to overcome financial ignorance while in a crisis that feels life threatening, like not having money for rent or food. I have worked with many of these folks, and I will say without a doubt that the complexities of poverty and getting out of it far exceed any investment question any multi-millionaire could bring me.

That said, wealth is also not without its complications and anxieties. With every step up the financial ladder, you take on greater responsibilities and risks. Each reward has tasks attached to it. I think it's like getting into shape: at first you just show up at the gym. The first workout may be filled with exhilaration that you did it. You are fuelled by a sense of direction and hope. By the third workout, muscles throb and it's a bit boring.

It takes a little while to reap the real benefits of the process, and each new step has new muscle aches attached to it, along with the ever-increasing health benefits and joy. It's the same for the money journey. Every step is fuelled by the wisdom gleaned from the previous one, so isn't as overwhelming as you may have feared.

When we go to Weight Watchers and they say, "It's not a diet, it's a new way of living!" we think to ourselves, "Whatever. I just want to lose the ten pounds." I often find in our classes that women want money to be a finite project with a clear-cut end point. Thinking that financial empowerment is a short-term set of tasks is very attractive to people new to the financial world, but the fact is that money is energy, and it's the fuel for our life. As long as we keep living, we're going to have to stay in relationship with it.

When we get to a destination we've always wanted to reach, we want to declare, "Wow, I just got to Seattle, great job!" and for short-term goals and projects that is exactly what we do: celebrate hitting a milestone, and that's good and right. But understand that we will always keep going on our money journey. We're either making progress in moving ahead or beginning the downward trip and falling behind—the dynamic nature of money will never let us stay still.

Temporary financial solutions are like fad diets. Every woman I know who tells me she's on some wacky diet will say, "I lost weight on it before!" Sure, but they've gained back the weight, and they are trying to use the same diet to fix the same problem that never really got fixed.

By this point in life, I know that to lose or stay the same weight requires constant attention—sustained effort. "Yo-yo dieting" is very similar to consolidating and paying off debt then maxing our credit cards all over again, or setting up accounting software on our laptop then not using it every month. It's a repetitive and discouraging cycle in which behaviours and thought processes at the root of the problem don't get addressed. So it is with money. We have to take the time to carve out a new and more functional relationship with it, learn the skills necessary to achieve our goals and find a tracking system that is manageable and allows us to monitor our progress.

A blueprint for finding solutions

There's a theory called "scaffolding" in developmental psychology, created by a researcher named Lev Vygotsky in the 1930s. He said many things about education, but the idea that I use when teaching about money is that once a person has ingrained a set of steps on how to solve one difficult problem, they've built a cognitive architecture that can be linked to or built upon, then used to solve other dissimilar problems. So, if you've been running a company for twenty years and you've got an aptitude for finding staff, you'll probably find you are just as able to assemble a trustworthy, competent money team.

If you've overcome adversity or fear in one situation, you can do it again in another. You have developed an innate architecture for solving those issues, learning those skills or mastering a competency. I ask people to call on those confidence areas to create new processes with their finances. You've succeeded before. You can succeed again. You have an internal blueprint just waiting to be called upon.

When you fully understand that the same kind of processes you've developed in other areas of your life can be applied to finances, you are on your way. We really do know where to begin; we just get the idea we don't, because of the false idea that money is so different from everything else—and it's not.

IT'S IMPORTANT to remember too that misinformation about finances is rampant in everyday conversation. At cocktail parties I hear things like, "You should pull out of the market now!"

or "What does your advisor charge for fees? Oh? Mine charges nothing." They are often exchanging information that is irrelevant and/or inaccurate, instead of asking interesting, useful questions, like "How did you fund your early retirement?" or "What are you teaching your kids about finances?"

People tend to talk about things that trigger emotion, like the situation in Greece or Israel. Most often, these events have no relationship to a person's family finances. World events are important in that we are all part of this planet, and we are all connected to each other. But at a purely practical level, if you have a laddered GIC portfolio at your local bank, these world events will have little impact on your financial well-being. Caring about the world is different than worrying about things that are both out of your control and unrelated to your life.

ANOTHER SKEWED idea is that money is separate from our values or that investing must be done in a way that causes some kind of harm (hurts the little guy or pollutes the planet), and this is just not true. Legitimate questions are: "How do I invest in a way that matches my values?" or "Am I losing money by investing according to my values?" Even better, you can articulate your values and ask for advice on how best to establish a plan or strategy that supports them. You may have values of independence, security, looking after parents. You may hold strong corporate values. For instance, any company I invest in must recycle and not use child labour. We want to have an aligned life where money, values and energy support our highest good.

I recently had an interesting dialogue with a well-known social activist. I challenged her by saying that from our conversation, I'd surmised she might not have the control over her personal finances that she should have. She became quite annoyed and said, "But I don't want unlimited money."

I had never said anything about unlimited money. I had only asked her to clarify something about her family finances and how they were keeping track of their cash flow. She seemed to be emotionally triggered by even the hint that we were talking about wealth building and preservation. She wanted to make an impact on her community and had dreams of becoming a philanthropist but was crashing into the "money is evil" wall.

When I ask women, "What do you want?" they typically answer with some variation of: lead a good life, have a happy family and get rid of belly fat (they don't actually tell me that, but I know they're thinking it.) At the root of this question is the source of what fuels all further discussion, plans and actions. The question speaks to self-worth and self-determination and gets right into the middle of the flames.

So, how do we get started on this financial planning journey? We begin by recognizing the resources we have, trying to shed light on our motivations and any impediments that may be getting in our way, and then having the courage to recognize that it is up to us to turn on the engine.

STEP ONE

WHERE
AM I NOW?

//////////////////////

THE PROCESS begins with finding out where you are, financially, at this moment.

We've been gearing up for this, and now it's time the rubber hit the road. This is the place where we do the most deep breathing. It is the simplest step, in the sense that everyone has to work with these concepts, every day, forever. Regardless of where we've been or how we got here, we get to look at where we are now. Today.

When I first began delivering financial education seminars, I used to ask people to do some homework. I would hand out the cash flow and net worth worksheets and ask them to fill them out before the next class.

It took a while before I realized that the drop-off rate between the first and second classes was very high. I would get calls like, "My mother is in the hospital and I need to go see her. In Greece." Or: "I lost my worksheet in the dryer." (You washed your worksheet?) Or my favourite: "I broke my thumb. Is it okay if I wait to do the homework until it gets mended?"

Being the astute psychologist that I am, I soon realized that the Step One of taking stock was rife with anxiety for most of the people taking my classes. I guess it's like the feeling we all get when we first step on the scale after Christmas. We are just not sure what we will find out, and the anxiety is unnerving.

Given that we need to take stock before we can get anywhere, this step can't be avoided, but we can change how we approach it. You might want to take a minute right now to go back and read about emotional mastery. And beliefs. And your socio-cultural upbringing. Take a deep breath and cut yourself a lot of slack. We can do this step without the mean stories and self-judgment and approach it with an air of curiosity and self-compassion instead. The heavy lifting here is not in the numbers or the lists or the data; it's at the level of moving through resistance. For some of us, it means moving out of the land of denial for the first time. For others, it means taking responsibility—for wealth or the lack of it. It doesn't matter where you are on the wealth continuum; if you have been avoiding knowing your financial situation, it might hurt a little to take this step.

The "Where am I now?" question in Step One has two parts: cash flow and net worth. They are related in that daily decisions about cash flow impact net worth. I think of cash flow as a snap shot and net worth as the photo album, or cash flow as the water droplets and net worth as the bucket they flow into over time.

CASH FLOW

Cash flow is essentially money in and money out. Money in can be salary, pensions, gifts, settlements, lottery winnings (we wish!), payments, contract fees, your roommates' share of the rent. Money out is the expenses you pay for. Your share of the rent, gas, food and purchases of any kind.

When we compare what is coming in with what is going out, we determine whether we have a surplus or a deficit. We can affect our cash flow dozens of times a day. Every financial decision we make, no matter how small, has an effect on our cash flow. It is also something we can affect immediately. If someone said, "I'm buying at the restaurant down the street, get anything you want, my treat!" that would immediately affect our cash flow. Cash flow is in the controllable realm, something we have complete authority over.

The most basic economic truth is that if we have more money flowing in than out, we have a positive cash flow. If we have more money flowing out than in, we have a negative cash flow. You can use fancy spreadsheets, online tracking systems or a notebook and pencil to follow this.

For the "newly awakened," I recommend keeping a notebook in your back pocket for one to three months to track every single thing you spend money on and every single thing that comes in. It will have a huge impact on your understanding of your personal decision-making and its effect on flow. We need to be conscious of where our money goes. This exercise wakes us up and makes us aware.

I can remember being so busy raising a family and working that I would sometimes stop and buy food at the grocery store on my way home from the office, having forgotten that I had already purchased a roast chicken on Saturday. I would discover the first chicken in the fridge at home. That's a symptom of being overworked and overtired and financially asleep.

I did the tracking exercise during my thirties for three years! I didn't start out with an ambition that large, but after tracking my spending for one month, I was taken aback by how much was going out but figured that month was unusual since it was my son's birthday and the furnace had to be repaired.

After three months of tracking, I was still shocked by the numbers but told myself that it was just a weird quarter as this was the time of year when our child care expenses were due and we also had that big car repair. So then I did it for a year and thought, well, that was a bizarre year; who would have thought we'd have so many medical issues?

It took three years before I felt that I fully understood and could own my own money story with authority. I was absolutely fascinated by my own spending behaviour and the way money worked in my life! (We should have known by then that a career change out of psychology was fast approaching for me.)

When I was growing up, I always felt like money was a mystery. It seemed there was a lot, then a little, then none, then more. I could never quite figure out why we were either on trips to Jamaica or eating rice and beans.

The biggest gift in this tracking exercise was earning a kind of emotional detachment. For the first time ever, I actually understood the flow of money in my life, and I liked the feeling.

I also saw that my spending was a window into my own values, both expressed and unrealized. Most of our money went towards the children. They had beautiful clothes, organic food and the best child care possible. Their father and I were dressed in secondhand clothes and drove old cars. When we saw how we were spending, we had a big discussion about our habits and values that was very illuminating. The fact was that we both wanted to spend our money in that way. Neither of us cared about cars or fancy dinners out, but we enjoyed the kids immensely. It all lined up well.

You might look at the flow at certain times and find that things are not so well in sync. It gives you the opportunity to say, "Stop. This is not my value system. I do not believe that deeply in café lattes."

This approach is a bit different from budgeting. I call budgeting one of the "B" words. It is similar to dieting and is a short-term fix that doesn't link to the deeper needs in one's soul. It causes all kinds of reactive behaviour. I like the word "flow." Put "cash" beside it and I find it quite sexy.

Money in, money out. It is a fundamental financial concept that can and should be altered to match the values of an individual. It is not about self-aggression or, even worse, denial or discipline. When we understand how something flows and we don't want it to flow that way, we can choose to set it on a different course—a much more powerful and effective framework.

How do you do this? Because I spent three years tracking expenses I ended up with a great Excel spreadsheet with every possible line item imaginable. I personally like financial details and a clear story so I wanted "inside home repair" separated from "décor" separated from "yard maintenance." Others may be more interested in simply using a line item like "home maintenance." Some people like tracking monthly or weekly. Some do it daily. It's a personal choice.

The biggest outcome of tracking cash flow is it wakes us up. I think most of us are walking around somnambulant—asleep at the wheel. We are just not aware of what we are actually doing and what it means. We are often cut off from reality because we are overly focused on reality. By that, I mean we are so hyper-conscious of the tasks that move us around each day, that we miss things like protecting the energy that fuels the tasks, or the values that fuel the beliefs that we need to do the tasks.

Money coming in is where we look at all the gifts and resources that flow into our lives. I think waking up here is also very powerful. Acknowledging that you make $50 every month in a gas rebate or by doing the neighbour's lawn or grabbing extra hours at work on a Saturday fills you with an appreciation of that income.

There are enough things written about the power of thankfulness, but I can't overstate how important it is. It is amazing how many gifts we possess. Taking stock of our blessings and giving thanks for them, whether they are in our cash flow or simply in breathing the air and drinking the clean water, helps us realize how much we really have.

Some days I consciously choose to look at all the wonderful gifts in my life. I focus on the flowers in my front yard, the mountains in the distance, the health of my kids and the clothes in my closet. These of course are happy, peaceful days. Then there are not-so-good shadow days, when I hear about people having things or experiences that I wish I had, and I slip into the illusion of not having enough. They trigger fear, insecurity and the very negative emotions that lead to spending weirdly and making irrational financial decisions. When we focus on lack, we end up creating more of it. This is a toxic pattern that I see in myself and in almost every human I know.

Sometimes when we take stock, we find that we may have clean water and great air and a roof over our heads, but there is more money flowing out than in. Even worse, this situation may have been happening for a long time. We may actually have debt. It might be a small debt proportional to how much we make or a shoulder-hunching, back-breaking, stomach-churning amount of debt. Being in debt often comes from a lack of resources and opportunities, but we can be in a negative cash flow situation even if we're a high-income earner.

SOME PEOPLE HAVE the biggest problem with the money-coming-in side of cash flow. This is where expenditures for improving income and increasing your job skills or negotiation ability can help. Some folks have the biggest trouble with the money-going-out side. They have patterns of spending that do not serve them. A whole book could be written about that alone. And many are.

When I hear the phrase "I deserve to…" I know a common compensatory overspending pattern is being revealed.

In my opinion, I don't think anyone "deserves" anything. A false sense of entitlement is rampant across all generations. The young do not have the market cornered on thinking that just by virtue of being alive and working hard, they are deserving of

Getting comfortable with surplus

WE ALWAYS NEED to be building capacity for wealth—creating a space within us for "the better." Every fortune has started with one dollar in surplus. Every millionaire started with that one dollar extra and was able to hold on to it and then grow it. If we can't handle surplus, we'll never become wealthy.

People who can't handle surplus come from a survivor-based mentality, usually within families who have lived in poverty or some kind of struggle, sometimes for generations. They feel that if they don't do something with their money right away, that opportunity is going to disappear. And their experience has supported that view.

This is also where you start building the "wealth muscle" of delayed gratification. If you can never wait for something or delay gratification, if you don't trust that you will ever get what you need or want, you will live in a moment-by-moment world of immediate rewards. You will never have surplus, and surplus is necessary to become an investor and to be financially secure. This is one of the major psychological underpinnings of debt and money problems. Delayed gratification is definitely a muscle that gets developed with practise over time. And again, I want to say that it's not about how much is coming in or going out; it's the relationship between the two that is important.

I've noticed in my pro bono work that people who are accustomed to being poor are very challenged to create surplus. Even if I have them keep a ten dollar bill taped to the fridge, they find that it creates tension. I have also learned that we all have a ceiling of surplus that we are wired for. For multi-millionaires it could be $50 million dollars. For a fourth generation welfare recipient it could be $20. This capacity needs to be stretched and strengthened to create an environment for more wealth to flourish. Even keeping a small amount as savings (in surplus) can lead to mammoth changes in self-concept, and this can lead to breakthroughs in increasing financial security.

When people have newfound wealth, many of them experience a psychological state called cognitive dissonance, in which our brain tries to rationalize two conflicting states or perceptions. We do not move to the middle ground. We either go towards one pole or the other.

You see this dynamic in lottery winners and people who suddenly inherit wealth. If someone receives money they didn't expect and don't have the skills or experience to deal with, they will use the new wealth in the characteristic way that they have always treated money. They may not have the capacity for surplus or delayed gratification or the ability to track their spending. So, having the money without the skills gets them nowhere new. They have to increase their capacity to deal with the large sum or they bring the large sum down to their capacity. Their bad habits just become bad habits with more zeros.

special treatment. Retirees on defined benefit pensions expect to live off the earnings of the young. They believe they deserve it—that their hard work entitles them to this gift.

You can earn it, save up for it, want it and maybe even need it, but *things* can't compensate for a lack of peaceful sleep or support or self-worth.

SOMETIMES THIS taking stock of cash flow step creates confusion. We start to over-think the process. Is it money out if it's an investment? Is it a debt if it's for college tuition? The answer is yes. Money in, money out doesn't change. It goes one way or the other. But money out can be smart and well thought out, or part of a plan for personal development or career enhancement and income growth. I hear questions like "Do I count new shoes for the suit I'm going to wear to a job interview? Isn't that an investment?" (By the way, I get this question a couple dozen times a year.)

Material goods like shoes or cars depreciate in value immediately upon purchase. They are not an investment. Things like career training, financial planning and educational classes are all good expenses in that you are investing in yourself in ways that can appreciate your value and your situation over time. But they are still in the money-out column.

A caution here about spending too much time navel-gazing and developing elaborate tracking systems: Beware the Fuss Factor. It can be paralyzing. Or the Blame Game, where it's everyone else's fault but your own.

We have to have a positive cash flow in order to move to the next steps in financial planning. A very logical way to make our cash flow positive is to make more and spend less, or some combination of the two. Don't over-complicate this step. It's simple although not always easy. It's the underlying personal issues demanding attention that create complexity and emotional reaction, not the process itself.

WHAT IS MY "NET WORTH"?

This is the second part of the Where Am I Now? step. Your net worth is everything you own minus what you owe. Your assets minus your liabilities. An asset is what you have; a liability is a debt. We aim to own more than we owe and have more assets than liabilities. As we discussed, shoes are neither an asset nor an investment, neither is the value of your term insurance policy. Your net worth is established for a living person, not your value to your relatives at your death.

I have found that most people don't know their net worth. This is especially common in women who are married for at least five years and have children. For better or worse, we all need to know where we stand. We need to see how the decisions we have been making daily, for years, have added up. We want to be able to create plans and strategies to achieve our cherished dreams, and to do that we need to know where we are today.

It takes courage to know the truth, but we need to know it, like it or not, whether we're in a negative situation or find ourselves flush.

Regardless of where you are now, in debt or with surplus, the truth is the truth. There's a simple beauty to that. A phrase I often use is: "It's okay. It is what it is." Kind of the Buddhist approach to wealth building.

These fundamentals aren't so much about the details of what we have, or judgments about it, but about being aware of what we have. It doesn't matter what our education or income is. We can be just as ignorant or educated about our finances as the next person—we just need to be awake and aware.

The first step in determining your net worth is to assemble and value your assets. The worth of your house, what your car would sell for today, the money in your RRSPs, savings in your bank accounts, all investment accounts, your share in the cottage, the diamond mine you own in Bolivia. Basically, anything that has enough value that you could sell it and receive money can be put into your asset list. I tend to stay away from adding up household effects. This list isn't for insurance purposes; it's to know where you stand at that moment.

Next, we assemble our liabilities. These are all the things we owe: credit lines, student debts, credit card bills, mortgages, personal loans, car loans. For each item, list the total owed, not your monthly payment amounts—those went into your cash flow summary.

Then we take all that we own and subtract all that we owe. The difference is our net worth.

Most people are surprised by the number. Many people say to me that they thought it was less or thought it was more. The number can be negative or positive, but it is the truth.

There are situations in which having a negative net worth can still be productive. If you have a mortgage or student loans, and you are working towards paying them off or are leveraging their value, you are on track with a plan. If your negative net worth is a temporary stepping stone to a bigger objective, it might still be appropriate for you to make certain kinds of investments—but there's no one-size-fits-all rule of thumb here.

STEP ONE TO-DO LIST:

Cash flow

- Choose a method for tracking your spending. There are several online programs you can use, or you can do it with a notebook and pen. Some people use Excel spreadsheets, and some buy software. Use whatever is easiest for you personally. There is no right way, only the right way for you. And that is the one you can sustain.
- Add up all your sources of money coming in by going through your bank statements or reviewing your tracking activity.
- Add up all your money going out.

· At the end of each month, subtract money going out from money coming in to determine whether you are in a state of positive or negative cash flow.

Net worth
· Add up everything you own that has monetary value: these are your assets.
· Add up everything you owe: these are your liabilities.
· Subtract your total liabilities from your total assets.

If the number is negative, then you are in debt. If your sum is a positive one, then you have a positive net worth. Bravo! You are either a capable investor or about to become one.

A note about debt

THERE IS WHAT we call "good debt" and "bad debt." Good debt has a plan and has an investment component attached to it: "I'm borrowing $10,000 against the equity in my house because I've always wanted to start a business, and I can pay it off in three to five years with the money I make in the business. Then I will triple my income." There's a plan. "I'm buying shelter because the money I make renting is adding up too much. It will control the amount of money I spend monthly and not be based on what a landlord *wants* me to pay." "I am going to get a student loan so I can get an extra year of education. ▶

That will move me up three steps on the pay scale at work, and I will make my money back four times over."

Bad debt has no purposeful reason for it and no road map to get out of it. It is based on consumer spending and gratification of wants that are out of line with income. Today, our society is carrying record levels of individual household debt. Constant changes in the economy are creating complexities that previous generations didn't encounter. Managing debt can be very challenging to handle alone, and I think there's a powerful internal stigma of failure, causing people to hide their money problems because they're so painful and humiliating to deal with. There's no magic formula, but there are warning signs that indicate problems are arising: making only the minimum payments on credit card balances, using cash advances to pay other credit cards, not knowing how much we owe and living paycheque to paycheque. Stress mounts, and that is tough at so many levels.

If your debt level is low, you may be able to reduce or eliminate it through a cash flow reassessment: adjusting your spending and/or income to put yourself in positive cash flow, eventually climbing out of the hole.

For people with serious debt who are unable to deal with their creditors on their own, debt management can be done with the help of a debt counsellor, money coach, insolvency specialist, bankruptcy trustee or credit counselling agency. There are many professionals that can assist and various legal options and strategies. We talk more about this in Chapter 11.

7

—— STEP TWO ——

DO I HAVE CASH RESERVE?

///////////////////////////

CASH RESERVE is money set aside for emergencies and opportunities. It is "liquid," which means you can access it in less than a day. A house is not cash reserve, and neither is an RRSP or your jewellery. It is the money that sits earning almost no interest in the bank. It is in a money market fund or a cashable GIC or simply a high-interest savings account. Because of its poor interest-earning potential, we don't want excess cash reserve—just enough to deal with unexpected occurrences.

The first question people ask about cash reserve is how much money they should put into it. I don't like formulaic answers. Hearing "I thought I was supposed to have equity allocation equal to 100 per cent minus my age" makes my eyes roll. They're handy little formulas, but they are mostly irrelevant.

Each of us has a different need for cash reserve, and it is based on our unique personal circumstances. If we have a stable career and live alone or with our parents, our cash reserve might not need to be so high. But if we are in the film industry and are responsible for three other people, that reserve will need to be higher. This is the first step that every single person needs to take to achieve financial freedom. I have seen cash reserves as low as $500 and as high as in the millions—the amount depends on the person, the relative amount of their wealth, their life responsibilities and availability of opportunities.

There are two main reasons we have cash reserve. One is very practical: having cash reserve means you reduce or eliminate the need to borrow. When a meteor falls through your roof, you don't have to use your Visa to remove the mess and repair the damage. When your best friend has a great deal on an investment property, you have the down payment handy. You can finance your own life.

I consider interest the penalty you pay for not having the foresight to build cash reserve. In its absence, you have to go outside of yourself and your resources to get the cash you will inevitably need. By the time you hit your late thirties, you begin to realize that "shit happens" and "life is full of surprises." This is a fundamental truth and speaks to the wisdom we have that the unexpected will occur and it will require funding. It is more secure and practical to take that money from your own reserve and then replenish it, and not pay the interest to the bank.

The second reason for cash reserve is that it has a strong psychological impact. With money set aside, a formal version of surplus, we feel brave and calm. And a calm mind is a well-functioning thinking and processing system. When we are in alarm and panic or some form of "fight or flight," our brain reverts to two main processing centres to handle what it perceives as an emergency. This may get us out of a war zone but doesn't allow us to do the lateral and creative thinking that our socially and financially complex world demands. In essence, cash reserve leads to superior decision-making.

Another question I get is "Should I build cash reserve even when I am trying to pay off debt?" When people decide they want to get out of debt, they think about paying all their debts off as quickly as they can to reach that goal. The common financial justification for this is that the interest rate is high on debt and low on cash reserve, so the economics would suggest that you should remove debt first.

And that sounds good, except for two things: One is that if you have an issue with holding on to surplus, we need to find out now before you engage in a three-year back-breaking debt removal exercise, only to start the whole cycle over again. We see this with people that successfully lose hundreds of pounds but have not built their skinny personality. They know how to lose weight but not how to be a person without a weight problem. This is the same with money. You need to practise being financially stable while you get rid of debt. You are building capacity then, and not just solving a financial problem.

Second, I have seen over and over again that when a person reaches the last or second-to-last payment of their debt, something negative happens. Remember: The unexpected must be expected. Just because you are paying off debt doesn't mean life stops—the meteor will find you, regardless. The Buddhists call this concept "Trouble at the border." Just before someone breaks through to a new phase, they meet resistance. In some ways, the "pushback" can even be a positive reinforcement of your hunch that you are taking a big step and moving forward. Trouble at the border, if you're not prepared for it, can be really discouraging. So, all along this journey, we need to set up contingency plans to prepare for this eventuality. There is going to be some resistance before every next life-changing step, be it in consciousness, finances, leadership or happiness, and you will encounter resistance. And it's *not* the universe telling you you're getting "too big for your britches"; it is just testing your resolve. It is your feedback mechanism that you are about to break free and step into something bigger.

A woman came in distraught two weeks ago. She had been working so hard to support her family and get her life on track.

She finally got the job she needed, and her kids were looking for jobs too. She was executing her financial rehab plan beautifully, and that month was going to be the first time she could pay all the bills that would come in. Then her ex-husband, who pays child support, called to say he had just lost his job and wouldn't pay child support anymore. She was beside herself. I reminded her about "trouble at the border" and that she had the capacity to handle this. We did some reframing and deep breathing. She emailed me back, saying that a bizarre thing had happened. She had just got another job offer at $20,000 more than her previous salary. She was going to be ahead of the game. These borders are to be celebrated and accepted and prepared for. Hence the need for building cash reserve and surplus while paying off debt.

TWO OTHER CONCEPTS related to the cash reserve step are protective gestures and capacity.

Protective gestures are the things we put in place to keep us safe when the unexpected or tragic occurs. Most of the time, a protective gesture is in the form of insurance or legal agreements or processes. If your net worth calculation came out negative, you may need insurance to support dependents if you should die or become disabled. You may find you need a co-habitation agreement because you saw that your fiancé has more debt than you or has a risky investment you do not want to participate in. These gestures create neutrality. They allow you to cope with misfortune without the additional burden of financial ruin for those we love and ourselves. They do not create a positive net worth, but they can prevent an even more serious problem from arising.

Take a look at the threats that could compromise your own situation and the people you care about. If you have a child with special needs and you should lose your job, what would your resources be? Make a cup of tea and jot down some possible challenges that you could face that are in the probable realm. You cannot insure yourself economically against every possibility, but you can take the top three or four threats off the list.

Capacity is the resources you have available to put towards growth. You have capacity when you have a positive net worth and you see that there is extra money in your bank account that can be invested in growing your assets. You could be building capacity before it might look like you are ready. When people use automatic payroll deductions to invest in RRSPs or use their company's contribution-matching program even while they have a negative net worth, they are building capacity.

Both are fundamental to financial planning. In my practise, I tend to deal with protective gestures and capacity first, before moving on to creating cash reserve.

STEP TWO TO-DO LIST:
Protective gestures
· Assess how much cash reserve you require by looking at your cash flow, the stability of your income situation and the probability of needing emergency or opportunity funding.
· Put a number to it.
· Assess the most probable threats to you and your family.
· Put a cost to them.
· Research the cost of putting protection in place against them.
· Decide whether it makes sense to insure this.

Building capacity
· Look at the opportunities for getting "free money" or "money at a discount" through employer programs at your workplace.
· Evaluate their impact on your finances now and the long term benefits.
· Put capacity-building actions into place where they make sense to you and will not harm your immediate cash flow to the point of creating debt.

8

WHERE
AM I HEADED?

/////////////////////////

We KNOW where we stand in terms of cash flow and net worth, and we have a reserve to fund opportunities and emergencies. Now we have earned the privilege of looking ahead and establishing goals. It is very telling that this step is the shortest written content of all the stages in this book, when it is the one most people spend the greatest amount of time talking about! It is the "little" chapter that falls between the two biggest pieces of work we do towards financial empowerment.

When I was employed as a financial advisor in the U.S., I would bring groups of women together to gather around our boardroom table for Oprah-inspired "visioning" classes. We had mounds of magazines and scissors and would create vision boards—the room alive with music and laughter and hope. All our dreams and goals and fantasies collected together on a piece of white bristol board. It was a blast!

But now I see that there is something kind of flawed about that process. It's okay to put pictures on a board, but it is not in the same universe as establishing real goals. As you have seen, financial planning is the marriage of *being* and *doing*.

In its essential form, this stage "Where am I headed?" has three pieces. First, set a goal. What is it you want? A new car? A new condo? A university education at Harvard? To retire in ten years?

Second, establish its cost.

And third, set a date you want to achieve it by.

When you put these three things together, you have a financial planning goal and have taken the first step of developing a realistic framework for achieving it. So, in short: set the goal, find out how much will it cost and establish the timeline.

I think that most of us can only really hold about three financial goals in our head at the same time. With too many, we become unfocused and overwhelmed and run the risk of falling back to sleep at the wheel or reverting to a kind of "magical thinking."

We could eventually have everything we desire, but it's a sequential process. Prioritizing allows us to focus, so that we can channel the appropriate energies needed for success. Our brain can only really concentrate on one thing at a time, and our financial security depends on making choices—great choices that support us. The choice-making skills you built in creating positive cash flow are further strengthened in setting goals. Choose the two or three things that really matter right now to get your focused attention and the full force of your mental, emotional and financial resources.

Some people really have trouble at this point. Moving from the "vision" to the actual belief that you can achieve a goal can set up some anxiety. Deciding on a goal, or two or three, and really thoughtfully committing to them can do exactly what it is intended to do—take the abstract and make it real. Doable. Probable. Now we are challenging any unconscious fears of failure or inadequacy, or that big one: unworthiness.

And those fears can come out swinging. We can be challenging a deep-seated idea that we are never getting anywhere or that anything more than survival is "too much."

For some, it is like holding onto surplus. Setting a few realistic goals may seem incredibly easy for some—but it is not easy for everyone.

Some of the shadows may look like cynicism, irritation, procrastination, or you may actually get bored to the point of sleepiness. You may need some help, like talking this through with someone or journaling about it. You may need to get every crazy thing you have ever wanted on a long list and then simply number them in order of importance.

One of the key reasons we set goals is to enable us to devise investment strategies. Each goal will have a very different investment strategy because of the cost and timeline for achievement. If we have $5,000, and the car we want is $10,000, and we want it within three years, the math will tell us that the compound rate of return needs to be around 26 per cent. What are the chances of getting 26 per cent for three years straight? Low to none. Now that we have that knowledge, we can choose a vehicle with a lower price tag or increase the timeline to purchase it or add savings. Instead of walking around saying "I never hit my goals," we might just need to rework our strategy for achieving them.

Say we need $100,000 cash to pay our Harvard tuition in seven years, and we have $60,000 saved up. We do the math or call our advisor, and we find out that we need to get 7.57 per cent each year. This again allows us to see whether there is an investment strategy we can use to achieve that or whether the goal needs to be modified in some way.

But here is the big difference between the rest of the world who are not financially savvy and us: we do the math at this point so that we know when and how to achieve our objectives.

We don't just randomly start devising portfolios or buying stocks in the hope that it will all work out. This stage is our first opportunity to make realistic high-quality choices and set a course for success.

The timeline is a big part of establishing strategy. You hear talk about goals that are short term (one to three years), mid term (three to five years) and long term (six years and up). This is where I see the most confusion among clients. Their goals don't match up with their strategies, given the timelines that they've chosen. But that's okay, because we are going to deal with that in the next step.

STEP THREE TO-DO LIST:
· Write a full list of all your goals.
· Attach a cost and date to each one.
· Assign a value of 1 to 10 to each goal, to indicate how much you care about it.
· Choose your top three.
· Move to the next planning step.

9

HOW DO I GET THERE?

A**T SOPHIA,** we use the term "wealth continuum." This is the pathway from being in debt to having surplus to protecting wealth once it has been achieved.

When cash flow and net worth are negative, the first job is to get that under control and to stop the money leak. Negative cash flow and/or negative net worth need to be acknowledged and a plan implemented to correct them, because like a water leak from the top floor of your house, they cause increasing damage the longer they continue.

We already talked about the ways we could deal with this, then about the neutralizing strategies or protective gestures that protect us from harm or catastrophe. These include legal agreements (wills, co-habitation agreements), formal processes (money tracking systems, schedules for advisory check-ins) and insurance (life or disability). We talked about creating surplus in the form of cash reserve. We also talked about debt and the importance of building cash reserve while paying off debt. These are all pre-investing steps.

This chapter addresses the wonderful situation where we have more surplus than we need for cash reserve, and we are wondering where to put it, what to do with it and how best to go about solving this dilemma. We are at the investing stage of the continuum.

Eventually, we will have earned so much in our investments that we will be at the far end of the investing scale. We will have assets that need protection, and we will look at strategies for minimizing taxes both in life and death. At that point, we are philanthropists looking for ways to share our wealth. We need a will and estate plan that reflect our understanding of tax and family values as well as the use of more complex insurance products that will help us protect our heirs. This is the stage of wealth preservation and legacy. We are graduates of the financial planning processes and have achieved a level of economic success that eludes so many. In a nutshell, this is the wealth continuum.

But let's not get ahead of ourselves. Before we can move forward, we need to figure out how we are going to use our surplus to achieve the goals we articulated in Step Three.

This is not going to be a how-to-invest chapter. It is going to be a how-to-understand-investing chapter.

I still believe that getting professional advice about the specifics is the best strategy for most people. The laborious process of creating portfolios and managing them yourself is time consuming, complex and, for most of us, unrealistic in light of our other responsibilities. Unless you have a personal passion for portfolio management and enough time in your life to devote to it, I believe it is simply foolish—and unnecessary—to take it on. But to fully understand the concepts of investing so that you can hire and supervise professional "sub-contractors" is an achievable and honourable goal. The market has become such a fast-moving, volatile environment that now more than ever we need to develop ways to oversee financial management by others for time efficiency, to reduce risk and for increased returns.

Risky business

RISK AS A word used in everyday language is synonymous with danger or a hazard. It is something to be avoided, stepped around or feared. It is one of the most over-used, misunderstood concepts in investing. In fact, I have recently seen it incorrectly defined on a government website.

Risk actually is a measure of the amount of uncertainty about the expected return of an investment. In financial terms, it is *not* a measure of the possibility that an investment might lose money or become worthless. In short, it is not a quantification of danger.

It is the variance of that investment in comparison to the average performance of the other investments of its type. In theory, an investment can be considered high risk even if it outperformed the other instruments of its class. You can see how this could get mixed up. It has a slight relationship to the human tendency to label things that are not fully understood, or are different, as "dangerous."

To make things even more confusing, there is also something called "risk tolerance." In precise terms, this quantifies the acceptable and unacceptable deviations from what is expected or the amount of ups and downs an investor can tolerate before committing hara-kiri. It is the term used to describe the degree of emotional discomfort an investor can tolerate in the midst of market volatility. In essence, it is really "risk appetite." Or the lack of.

You can also be "risk averse," which means you want to avoid risk regardless of the consequences. If you recall from Chapter 4, women do better at managing risk when they are fully apprised of the consequences of their decisions. The more educated they are, the better able to withstand higher levels of risk they become. Men are the opposite.

Picture this common scenario. A woman sits with an advisor as they walk her through one of those online financial questionnaires. The advisor asks questions like "How do you feel about losing money?" and "How would you react if your investment depreciated in the next three months?" Now how does an intelligent woman respond? "Badly! I wouldn't like it!" That's because we have a brain. No one wants to lose money.

But unfortunately, because of the use of the word "risk" in these simple questionnaires, women are often inaccurately categorized as "conservative" investors. This is particularly prevalent in banks and credit unions.

In general, as much as I like and respect my banker friends (as a banker's main objective is to always get their money back!), they would have become a professional poker player or perhaps a race-car driver if they had any appetite for risk. At a bank or credit union, you are quite likely to be talking to someone who has a disproportionate amount of GICs in their own retirement accounts. I know this from experience because, I have seen this in actual portfolios.

So, *potentially*, you have someone doing a risk assessment on you who personally has low tolerance for risk. In addition, the people who made up the questionnaires ▶

to mitigate any potential liability are likely to be biased towards risk aversion as well. In any case, be careful how you answer these questions. If need be, ask more questions before you answer.

An aggressive investor, or one with a high risk tolerance, is more likely to accept the idea of temporary declines in the value of their assets in order to get better results in the long term. They are willing to sacrifice certainty and are willing to wait. In essence, these investors train themselves to manage fear and strong emotion and are often compensated with greater returns.

Conversely, a conservative investor, or one with a low risk tolerance, will favour investments that will preserve the original investment. They would rather have certainty than the possibility of a high return. They may also have no need for accepting volatility, as they may have reached their financial goals already and therefore no longer have to expose their money to the ups and downs of the stock and bond markets.

Matching the emotional capacity for tolerating volatility (risk) with the level of risk required to reach your goals is the fundamental task in developing appropriate and effective investment strategies. In some cases, building a woman's capacity for risk or volatility may be essential for her long-term security. Understanding the repercussions of not taking on risk (like running out of money at age 74) may be motivation enough for learning to tolerate a "wilder ride."

We tend to do what is necessary if we understand why an action or behaviour is required.

TYPES OF ASSETS

There are three basic asset classes:

1. Cash and cash equivalents
2. Fixed income (or bonds)
3. Equities (or stocks)

Here are their definitions.

1. **Cash and cash equivalents.** Cash is exactly what you might think it is: money in your savings account at the bank. Examples of cash equivalents are redeemable Guaranteed Investment Certificates (more commonly known as GICs), treasury bills, money market accounts and short-term deposits.

They are the safest investments but usually offer the lowest return of the three major asset categories. The chances of losing money on an investment in this asset category are extremely low. The federal government guarantees many investments in the cash equivalent category. Investment losses in non-guaranteed cash equivalents do occur but infrequently.

The biggest worry for investors with cash equivalents is that inflation will outpace the interest they are receiving on their deposits and create a long-term negative growth situation. The purpose of cash in a portfolio (as opposed to the cash reserve you have set aside for opportunity and emergencies) is to provide a strong, safe, stable foundation for your portfolio.

2. **Bonds or fixed income.** Companies and governments offer bonds to raise money. When you buy a bond, you are lending your money to a company or government for a set period of time—typically anywhere from a year or less to as long as 30 years. When that time comes to an end, it's called a bond's "maturity date." On that day, the company or government that borrowed your money is supposed to pay it back in full. This amount is called the "face value" of the bond. You make money

from a bond in two ways: you either hold it for the full term and continue to receive the set rate of interest for lending your money, or you sell the bond before it reaches maturity. You can make money or lose money, depending on what the current bond market is like.

There are many kinds of bonds to choose from, issued by many sources: federal government bonds, Crown corporation bonds, provincial government bonds, municipal bonds (by cities), Corporate (from public corporations) bonds.

Essentially, because you are lending your money out, there are some risks involved. You could lose money if you need to sell the bond before it matures and the market values your bond as worth less than what you paid for it. This happens when the interest rates on new issues of bonds are higher than when you purchased it. Or you may not get your money back at all if the company or government that issued the bond goes broke or out of business.

This type of risk varies a great deal, because some companies and governments are more stable than others. The higher the probability that you may not get your money back, the higher the rate of interest you will probably receive. If a company that issues a bond goes bankrupt, there is a chance you might not get your money back, but there is generally less risk of losing all your money than there is if you owned stock in the same company. That's because in the case of insolvency, people who hold bonds get their money ahead of people who own the company's stock.

One way of reducing risk is to buy bonds that mature on different dates. This is known as "bond laddering." This can help you reduce the impact of changing interest rates, which in turn affects the salability of a bond.

Very high-yield bonds are sometimes called "junk bonds." They can offer superior returns and help boost your income. Or they can be companies on the verge of going under—junk—and you might lose your capital. You need an expert to help you discern which is which. Sophisticated investors can get very wealthy investing in these low-grade bonds. Or they can go broke.

Bonds with long maturities also usually offer higher interest rates. This is because there is just no way of knowing where interest rates will go over a long period of time or how stable the company will be in thirty years. If interest rates go up, the price of your bond will fall, because the interest rate is lower and therefore less desirable than the new bonds being issued at the higher interest rate.

In the fixed income category are also **non-redeemable GICS** (Guaranteed Investment Certificates as sold in a bank or credit union.) They are low, low risk because they are guaranteed, but they behave like bonds, as they have one-to-five-year maturities and offer predetermined interest rates and durations.

3. **Equities (or stocks).** Historically, these have had the greatest volatility and highest returns among the three asset categories. Companies sell stock (a piece of ownership) on the stock market to get money to help fund business growth. Investors can buy stocks from a financial advisor that is licensed through IIROC. They can either go to a full service broker or to a discount broker.

As an asset class, stocks are a portfolio's Olympic athletes, offering the greatest potential for "winning" growth. Stocks sometimes get gold medals but also sometimes fall off the track and don't even place. The volatility of stocks makes them an inappropriate short-term investment. Large-company stocks as a group, for example, have lost money on average about one out of every three years. And sometimes the losses have been quite dramatic. But investors who are willing and able to ride out the volatile returns of stocks over long periods of time generally have been rewarded with strong positive returns.

The stock market brings together people who want to sell with those who want to buy. It is inherently a big conflict-based system, with one side believing something is worth buying and the other side believing it is not, and then both negotiating the best price. This is done electronically through **stock exchanges**.

Many factors affect the price of a stock. In simple terms, a stock's price rises when there are more people wanting to buy a stock than there are people who want to sell it. People compete to buy a stock if they believe that the price of the stock will rise and they will make a profit. A stock's price falls if there are more people who want to sell a company's stock than there are buyers. Sellers compete to offer the lowest price to the buyers.

When experts choose stocks for a portfolio, they look at various fundamentals. They look at the company's balance sheet to see if there are enough assets to cover liabilities that the company owes. If a company is short on cash, this may be a warning sign. They look at the track record of growth. If a company is young and has no track record, there is considerably more risk. Experts review a company's operating statements and leadership. They evaluate the reputation of the leadership team and their performance at other companies. They study the factors that could affect its performance and its future growth, and they might look at the dividend (payout) history.

There really is no surefire investment in the stock market. Economic and market trends can affect the price of even a good stock. But in a free market economy, the general belief is that the market will price the company fairly...eventually.

UNDERSTANDING ASSET ALLOCATION

Asset allocation is the proportion of cash, fixed income and stocks chosen for a portfolio. And remember, you can have several portfolios, each with a different goal and time horizons. And each requires a different formula.

Choosing our asset allocation—creating our own personal blend from the three asset classes—is critical to safe and suitable investment management. It is how we ensure that the investments in our portfolios don't all go up or down at the same time. Each asset class has historically performed differently, with different triggers for going up or down and different long-term rates of return.

It is also highly related to the concept of diversification. You've heard the expression "Don't put all your eggs in one basket." That's the underlying fundamental of having different asset classes. The assumption is that over time we are protecting ourselves from wild swings or huge losses by making sure that our investments are well balanced. The main purpose of asset allocation is to help manage volatility (the ups and downs).

By including asset classes with investment returns that move up and down under different market conditions within a portfolio, an investor tries to protect themselves against significant losses. Historically, the returns of the three major asset categories have not gained and lost at the same time. Market conditions that cause one asset category to do well often cause another asset category to have average rates of return or to lose value. Interest rates, new tax laws and political or economic upheaval can all affect how an asset class behaves. By investing in more than one asset category, you'll reduce the chance that you'll lose money, and your portfolio's overall investment returns will have a smoother ride. If one asset category's investment return falls, you'll be in a position to counteract your losses there with better investment returns in another asset category. At any given time, you should have one class of investments that is doing well, regardless of market conditions.

Wise asset allocation is important because it plays a major role in determining whether you will meet your financial goals. If you don't include enough volatility or growth investments in your portfolio, your investments may not earn enough to meet your objectives. For example, if you go back to Step Three of your plan and see that in one of your goals you need a 5.5 per cent rate of return to achieve it, you will not be able to do so with only cash in the portfolio. On the other hand, if you know you will need to get your money out in three years, you wouldn't want to have all your money in stocks. If that three-year period happens to be a particularly volatile time in the stock market, your investments may not be at a good price when it comes time to sell, and you may not hit your target.

Determining the appropriate asset allocation model for a financial goal is a complex task. Basically, you're trying to pick the mix of assets that has the highest probability of meeting your goal at a level of volatility you can stomach. As you get closer to meeting your goal, you'll want to adjust the mix of assets to reflect the shorter time horizon.

TIME HORIZON AND DIVERSIFICATION

When my daughter, who has attended numerous financial classes, tried to get a mutual fund portfolio with 90 per cent equities, she was refused by her local bank account representative. She told him, "But I have a 40-year time horizon!" (Good girl!) He told her she was too young to have this "risky" an asset allocation. It seemed incredibly illogical. How can you be too young to have volatility? When do you actually get to make money?

My daughter had answered the questions thoroughly and thoughtfully, and even with a good understanding of what she was doing, the banking system was skewed in favour of the more conservative GICs and bond funds. We had to get the bank manager involved.

Time horizon is the 40 years my daughter had before she thought she might need her money. It is exactly what it sounds like: the expected number of weeks, years or decades you have allotted to achieve a particular financial goal. An investor with a longer time horizon may feel more comfortable taking on a more volatile portfolio, because they have the time to wait out the ups and downs of the market and economic expansion and recovery cycles. By contrast, an investor saving up for a cross-border hip operation would probably take on less volatility, because of the shorter time horizon and the necessity for the money to be there at a specific time.

Diversification is simply the "eggs in the basket" concept. A diversified portfolio should be diversified at two levels: between asset categories and within asset categories. So, in addition to distributing your investments among stocks, bonds, cash equivalents and possibly other asset categories, you'll also need to spread out your investments within each asset category. The key is to classify investments in segments of each asset category that may perform differently under different market conditions. So, not only do you want to spread your eggs across different baskets; you want to make sure each of those baskets contains a variety of egg types.

One of the ways of diversifying your investments within an asset category is to identify and invest in a wide range of companies and industry sectors. Examples of industry sectors include manufacturing, consumer goods, and oil and gas. But the stock portion of your investment portfolio won't be diversified, for example, if you only invest in one or two companies. We think you need at least 16 carefully chosen individual stocks to be truly diversified. This means that in today's world it might take about $150,000 before you can get proper diversification in a specific stock portfolio. Because achieving the right level of diversification can be so challenging, some investors may find it more efficient to use mutual funds.

A **mutual fund** is a company or investment that pools money from many investors and invests the money in stocks, bonds and other financial instruments. Mutual funds make it easy for investors to own a small portion of many investments, even if they have only a small amount of money to invest. A **total stock market index fund**, for example, owns stock in hundreds of companies. As an individual investor, you would need significant capital to assemble such a diverse portfolio.

An equity mutual fund lets you invest in a group of stocks chosen by a professional fund manager. Often you can have access to a broader range of investments than you could buy on your own. When you put your money in a mutual fund along with many other people, it creates a large pool of money that can be invested. You then own proportional units of that fund. You don't actually own pieces of the underlying securities (stocks) but pieces of the fund.

If the investments in the fund do well, the price of your units will go up, and you will make money when you sell. If they are not doing well, the unit price drops. You will lose money if you decide to sell your units when the price is down. In some cases, the money the fund makes will be distributed to its investors in the form of cash or additional units.

The advantage of a mutual fund is that they are an affordable way to get diversification and professional management. Be aware, however, that a mutual fund investment doesn't necessarily provide instant diversification, especially if the fund focuses on only one particular industry sector. If you invest in narrowly focused mutual funds, you may need to invest in more than one mutual fund to get the diversification you seek. Within asset categories, that may mean considering, for instance, large company stock funds as well as some small company and international stock funds. Between asset categories, that may mean considering stock funds, bond funds and money market funds.

Mutual funds are "liquid" in that they can be redeemed at the end of each trading day. They can also provide automatic reinvestment of the cash or units of the distributions mentioned above.

Types of mutual funds

THE COMPANY THAT runs the mutual fund appoints a fund manager, who operates the fund under a mandate, which is the description of what the manager will invest in and the parameters of the holdings. This is outlined in the prospectus, which is a formally written, legal document. A manager may have been given the mandate to operate a Canadian balanced fund that never exceeds 40 per cent bonds or an international mandate that can only invest in companies in countries in Europe. It spells out what the investor will be investing in by owning that fund. Within this mandate, the fund manager decides where to invest the money and makes all buy and sell decisions.

There are eight common types of mutual funds:

1. **Money market** funds invest in very safe, short-term investments such as government bonds, bankers' acceptances and treasury bills. This is like a mutual fund of cash and cash equivalents that generally pays 1 to 2 per cent more than a savings account. It is highly liquid, and your money can be accessed in under a day. It can be a great place to store your cash reserve.

2. **Fixed income** funds buy investments that pay a fixed rate of return. These funds invest in short-term, medium- and long-term bonds and debentures (this is like a bond but with no collateral backing it except the reputation of the issuer) of federal, provincial and municipal governments, as well as major corporations and mortgages. The aim of a bond fund is to provide investors with maximum interest income and growth from buying and selling bonds. ▶

The difference between owning a bond fund and holding individual bonds is that with a bond fund there is no maturity date and no promised repayment of the cash you invest.

3. **Balanced** funds run the gamut. They invest in a mix of stocks, fixed income and money market investments. These funds try to balance out growth and volatility to maximize your gains while attempting to increase stability of returns. Most of these will follow a mandate that spells out the percentage of cash, bonds and stocks the manager can hold. This helps you determine the level of volatility of the fund and where it fits in your investment strategy.

4. **Stock** funds are also known as **equity** funds. They invest in a variety of stocks. Usually this is further outlined in the prospectus by country, size of the company and what kinds of sectors they are in, and they may even have additional descriptions like "socially responsible" or "high growth." The words large, mid or small "cap" (capitalization) are often used to describe companies. Market capitalization is calculated by multiplying the number of a company's shares outstanding by its stock price per share. Large cap companies will have a track record of growth that extends over years, and small cap may be younger companies that show promise. The less of a track record, the more uncertain the investment and the greater possibility of a large reward. Or loss.

5. **Index** funds match the holdings and changes of a certain market. The value of the units in the fund will change, rising and falling as the exchange index goes up or down. There are thousands of index funds available. These funds

may track a whole index or just a selection, like the S&P/ TSX 60, which tracks only the 60 biggest companies on the Toronto Stock Exchange.

6. **Specialty** funds focus on investing in a certain industry or category (e.g., high tech or socially responsible) or in a certain part of the world, or they may only buy precious metals or companies from developing countries (the "emerging" market). These funds can have the potential of very high returns or losses and are part of a larger overall investment strategy and not usually the sole holding for an investor.

7. **Mortgage** funds are a diversified pool of mortgages that typically hold conventional mortgages, including residential, industrial and commercial. But some may hold more precarious mortgages to increase the return. The fund might also invest in government bonds or hold cash. The objective of mortgage funds is typically to create income for investors from the payments the mortgage holders make.

8. **Real estate** funds invest in Real Estate Income Trusts (REITs). REITs invest in properties that earn income, like shopping malls and commercial buildings.

   In addition, **Exchange Traded funds** (ETFs) allow an investor to buy an entire portfolio of stocks through a single security that tracks and matches the returns of a stock market index. ETFs, like mutual funds, offer people a way to pool their money in a fund that makes investments in stocks, bonds or other assets, and, in return, to receive an interest in that investment pool. Unlike mutual funds, however, ETF shares are listed and traded on an exchange and trade like a stock. ▸

Certain ETFs can be relatively easy to understand. Other ETFs may have unusual investment mandates or use complex investment strategies that may be more difficult to understand and fit into an investor's investment portfolio. So, beware. They are an economical way to participate in a market without holding individual securities and often have very low management fees (management expense ratios, or MERs for short). Some are considered a passive investment, like an index fund, and mirror the volatility of the market they represent.

WHAT ABOUT FEES?

There is so much written about fees in the media. And I'd like to caution you against spending too much time on this. Because fees are a simple mechanism for decision-making, investors who focus too closely on them often overlook more important characteristics like the track record of the manager, quality of the fund and, most importantly, its role in your portfolio. Frankly, I see this emphasis on fees used too often as a way to simplify investment decision-making.

Of course we want as low a fee as possible for a high-quality instrument, but beware of using this as a primary decision-making criterion. I think sometimes it's one of the few things people understand, and so they focus on this to gain a sense of being in control and savvy when really they may have lost out on a beautiful investment with a higher fee that would make them far more money with lower volatility over the long run. It's just one of several criteria that should be used for evaluating your investment.

Here's how to decipher the fees in a mutual fund you are considering buying.

The fund manager gets a fee from the fund for making allocation and investing decisions. A management expense ratio (MER) covers fees paid to the advisors who sell the fund; bookkeeping, legal, audit and administrative fees; as well as the costs for filings with the provincial securities commissions. The MER is charged against the fund and not the investor directly. The returns are quoted net of fees, which means they are calculated after the expenses have been taken out. Commissions, or "loads," however, are charged directly to the investors. There are three types of loads:

1. **Front End Load or Initial Sales Charge (ISC).** Some advisors charge a fee when you purchase a fund from them. This is a percentage of the amount that you are investing in the fund, for example, 2 per cent.

2. **Back End Load or Deferred Sales Charge (DSC).** A fee that is charged when you sell units of the fund. The longer you hold a fund with a DSC, the less you will be charged when you sell it. It would be typical for this charge to run out between five and seven years. Advisors are paid very well when they sell these funds because the idea of being charged to sell tends to feel like a penalty and will often lead to longer holding periods for clients. The downside is that with the constant changes in mutual fund managers and performance, investors often feel they can't afford the charge and ironically end up losing more money by holding on to a failing fund. I personally don't like the psychology of this kind of sales charge, nor do I like the behaviour it inspires in advisors or investors.

3. **No Load** funds do not charge when you buy or sell units. But it is important to look at the MER, because sometimes the internal costs are higher than if you had paid an up front load.

MANY MARKETS

I try not to feel exasperated when someone approaches me and says, "Wow, how about that market, eh!" indicating that they have had CNN on today. I always ask, "What market?" By most estimates, approximately 630,000 companies are now traded publicly on over 100 stock exchanges around the world, with the U.S. having the largest exchange, the New York Stock Exchange (NYSE). Not only are there many stock markets, but there are bond markets, commodities markets, currency and gold markets and a myriad of others.

Each one of these markets can be tracked by an **index**. A market index tracks the performance of a specific "basket" of holdings considered to represent a particular market or sector of a market. There are **indices** (or indexes) for almost every conceivable sector of the economy and stock market. Many investors are familiar with these indices because they have heard of index funds and **exchange-traded** funds whose investment objectives are to track the performance of a particular index.

An index is a commonly accepted way to look at the performance of a group of investments. It is called a benchmark when it is used to measure the performance of an investment against others like it. So, if you had a basket of fruit in your shopping cart and someone asked you for the calorie count, you would simply add up the various caloric values and create an average for a piece of fruit, in general. But we know that an individual banana may have quite a different count than a piece of watermelon. Still, it enables us to get a picture of the overall "fattening quotient" of the fruit in the cart. We can then measure the value of the individual piece against the whole. Likewise, if one shopping cart had fruit and the other had baked goods, it would also allow us to compare the two carts against each other by looking at the averages within them.

To some degree this is also the principle behind asset

allocation. We may have three shopping carts, each with a different class of food in it, and we figure out how much we need of each to hit the right calorie count for that day. Each person needs a different calorie count and even may want to have high-calorie and low-calorie days, so it is not a one-size-fits-all plan, nor can it necessarily be the same for years at a time.

There are several stock markets and stock market indexes that you may have heard of:

· **S&P/TSX Composite Index** comprises the majority of Canadian-based publicly traded Toronto Stock Exchange listed companies. It is the leading benchmark in Canada and is used to measure the price performance of the broad Canadian senior equity (blue chip or older, larger) market. It was formerly known as the TSE 300 Composite Index.

· **S&P/TSX Venture Composite Index** was launched December 10, 2001, and is the leading benchmark used to measure the price performance of the Canadian public venture capital equity (stock) market. These companies are "new venture," which means they are very young, very small and unproven, and are often in their first round of raising capital. They are sometimes called "micro-caps" to indicate that they are even smaller than small cap companies.

· **Dow Jones Industrial Average (DJIA)** was introduced in 1896 by Charles Dow as a way of gauging market health. He simply took the average price of twelve specific stocks. Now more than a hundred years later, the DJIA is more complex. Since 1928, the index has comprised 30 blue chip stocks as selected by the editors of the *Wall Street Journal*. These blue chips are well established, recognized companies that sell high-quality, widely accepted products and services.

· **Standard and Poor's 500 Index (S&P 500)** is made of the largest 500 U.S. corporations. The index was introduced on March 4, 1957, and was the first computerized stock index. The companies in the S&P 500 are selected by a committee, then each stock is weighted according to the company's market value. Though the Dow Jones is more well known, the S&P 500 is considered a more accurate representation of American overall market performance.

· **The Nasdaq Composite** is heavily weighted in technology and Internet stocks. The Nasdaq Composite dates back to 1971 and was the world's first electronic stock market. The more than 3,000 companies listed in the composite are considered to have high growth potential and tend to be more speculative and risky than those listed on the NYSE. Because of this, the Nasdaq Composite Index is much more volatile than other indexes.

· Other international stock market indexes you may have heard of are: London's **FTSE 100**, France's **CAC40**, Germany's **DAX 30**, Japan's **Nikkei 225**, **MSCI EAFE** (an index of non-Canadian or U.S. stocks), U.S.'s **Wiltshire 5000** (meant to measure the entire U.S. stock market.)

Bond market indexes are also numerous and varied. A few on a very long list are: the **RBC Canadian Bond Market Index**, the **DEX Universe Bond Index** and the **DEX Short-term, Mid-term and Long-term bond indexes**, and the **FTSE Global Bond Index Series** or the **FTSE NSE Kenyan Shilling Government Bond Index Series**.

WHAT DO I PUT MY MONEY INTO NOW?

In class, I often explain this next step as a house on a cul-de-sac surrounded by other houses. Each one has a slightly different porch and roof line and is made of different materials on the front-facing wall. These differences affect how each is viewed and valued. But the furniture items that go into each of the houses are basically the same. You can put a couch, chair or table in any of the houses.

I liken the houses to the different investment vehicles or mechanisms you can use to hold your investments. You have chosen an appropriate asset allocation structure. You have determined whether you are using stocks, bonds or cash or whether at this point you need mutual funds for diversification. You know the proportions of each asset class you want to meet your goals, time horizon and risk tolerance. We now turn our energies to figuring out whether you are going to use registered or non-registered "houses" for your "furniture."

Registered investment plans

A **registered investment account or plan** is a legal agreement between you and the Canada Revenue Agency that a certain tax structure will be used for that house of investments. When it is registered, there is a tax-sheltering component that motivates people to use that plan. The consequence is you have to follow a set of rules.

· A **Tax-Free Savings Account (TFSA)** allows you to earn income or growth of your money without paying taxes. Canadian residents aged 18 or older who have a valid Social Insurance Number (SIN) can contribute to a TFSA up to a set limit each year. The key benefit is that you do not have to pay any taxes on anything you earn within the account (including interest, dividends or capital gains) or on money you withdraw from the TFSA. But your contributions to the account are not tax-deductible. You can carry forward any unused contribution room for years, and you can withdraw your money to use it for any purpose.

Although these have been touted as great savings vehicles, I often wonder why. They are great accounts to put in our highest growing, greatest-interest-bearing investments because of their

How to ask for what you want

ONE OF THE things that prevents us from feeling in control and confident about our financial life is not knowing how to speak about money when we communicate with an advisor. It helps to use the right language because it helps you be clear about what you are doing and asking for. The correct language for setting up a registered plan is simply: "I'd like to open an RRSP" (or TFSA). Or "I'd like to contribute to my RRSP" (or TFSA). Again, you do not "buy an RRSP," because it is a *structure*, not the actual investment. I have seen this incorrectly referenced in newspapers and heard it from the mouths of undertrained bank employees.

ability to grow money without paying taxes on the growth. But why would you use these for saving? Just use a high-interest savings account for that purpose.

Inaccurately again, it is often advertised that you can "buy a TFSA." Banks and credit unions that use this language really mean you can *set up* a TFSA and *buy* a term deposit or GIC to be held within the TFSA. But again, why? With interest rates so low, why not save yourself the hassle and use a savings account for savings and the TFSA for growing? When you withdraw your money, it can be used for any purpose.

· A **Registered Education Savings Plan (RESP)** can be opened as soon as a child is born. The money in the plan grows tax-free, and the government offers special savings incentives. When a child enters a qualified post-secondary educational program they can start withdrawing the accumulated savings. The child pays taxes on the growth of the money that is withdrawn. Since many students have little or no other income, they usually don't have to pay much tax when they withdraw the money for school.

When you contribute to an RESP, the government of Canada will supplement your deposit with a Canada Education Savings Grant, which allows you to accumulate money faster. The amount of the grant depends on your contribution and family circumstances. The government provides more help for families with low or modest income and may include an enhanced Canada Education Savings Grant and a Canada Learning Bond, which provide additional motivation and assistance to those families who want their children to receive a post-secondary education but may be challenged to afford it.

· A **Registered Retirement Savings Plan (RRSP)** is the most well know of the registered plans. They were introduced in 1957 and were intended as a way to encourage savings for retirement by Canadian employees.

There are a variety of restrictions laid out in the Canadian Income Tax Act with these accounts. You can withdraw money from your RRSPs at any time, but you will have to pay taxes on what you withdraw. These taxes are at your personal income tax rate at the time of withdrawal. RRSPs are designed to be a long-term savings tool to help you save for retirement. Unless you have no other options available, you should not withdraw from your RRSP until retirement. Because of the tax benefits provided by RRSPs, the government has capped the amount of money that can be contributed annually.

Just to make things confusing, sometimes the contribution limit is called the "deduction limit," which actually makes sense, since the two defining characteristics of an RRSP are that you make a contribution and get a tax deduction. At the time of the writing of this book, Canadians are allowed to contribute 18 per cent of their yearly earned income, or a maximum of $23,800 in 2013 (whichever is the lesser amount), to their RRSPS. You can contribute to an RRSP on any business day throughout the entire year, even though the bank lines in February might have you thinking differently! To get a deduction on your taxes on this year's return, the deadline is the first 30 days of the following year. Unused contribution room can be carried over from year to year.

THERE ARE many opinions about whether to use an RRSP or just a regular investment account (non-registered) to save for retirement. Some advisors suggest that since only 50 per cent of capital gains (the amount you sold something for minus what you paid for it) are considered taxable income, it is better to keep the flexibility of a non-registered account and pay higher taxes up front.

The choice between an RRSP and non-RRSP investment is fast becoming one of the most debated issues in the financial community. Some advisors point out that RRSP withdrawals are fully taxed as income at rates of up to 49 per cent—versus capital gains, where only half the gain is taxed at an individual's tax rate. To generate mostly capital gains and take advantage of the lower tax rate, they suggest simply investing in a non-registered account with long term appropriate investments, like the stocks and bonds and mutual funds we talked about.

But that said, RRSPS still make sense for most people. Because of tax-deferred compounding of all types of income within an RRSP, it is difficult to beat the amount that may be accumulated within a registered plan over time. As well, the psychological reward of socking away money and not paying tax in the short term probably increases the amount people allot to savings. To me, this is the biggest advantage and most difficult to quantify. How much would you put away if you didn't get a tax break on this year's return? How much would you put away knowing you are getting a reward for this behaviour?

How RRSPS stand up against non-RRSPS will vary from person to person, based on a few factors like their investment return and tax rates, now and at retirement or withdrawal. Obviously, if you are going to have a high or higher income at retirement (as is the case with several of our clients), it may simply not be worth the hassle. But recent tax changes now allow retirees over the age of 65 to transfer up to 50 per cent of their RRIF and other pension income to their spouse or common-law partner. This form of income splitting can potentially save a couple a significant amount in taxes.

To help you make the best decisions for your situation, look at a number of scenarios, taking into account all aspects of your personal financial plan. You may need a professional to work with you on this.

There are two exceptions where you can withdraw from your RRSP tax-free:

· The **Home Buyers Plan (HBP)** where you can borrow up to $25,000, tax-free, from your RRSP for a down payment on your first home. You must re-contribute the money to the RRSP within 15 years.

· **The Lifelong Learning Plan (LLP)** lets you borrow money from your RRSP to help you pay for education or training for you or your spouse. You cannot use the borrowed money to pay for the education of your children or your spouse or common-law partner's children.

Other registered funds include:

· The **Registered Retirement Income Fund (RRIF)** kicks in at age 71, when you are no longer allowed to contribute to your

RRSP. At this point, you have two options: You can transfer your RRSP savings into either a Registered Retirement Income Fund (RRIF) or an **annuity** (a purchased investment that guarantees income). You could also withdraw the full value of your RRSP, but this would mean paying taxes on the whole amount. A RRIF allows you to withdraw your RRSP savings as income for retirement.

Similar to an RRSP, the funds within an RRIF can be held and grow tax-free, and you can choose the types of investments you hold. Every year, after your 71st birthday, you have to withdraw a minimum amount from your RRIF. Right now, the minimum amount is about 7.5 per cent at age 71, with the minimum amount gradually increasing to about 20 per cent by age 94. You can choose how much you would like to withdraw in excess of these minimums and how often you receive payments. Keep in mind that the larger the withdrawal, the more tax you will pay.

· The **Registered Disability Savings Plan (RDSP)** is an investment option offered to families for relatives with disabilities to help them save for long-term care. This plan allows the account holder to invest up to $200,000 in a tax-deferred account on behalf of a disabled recipient. To be eligible, the beneficiary (a legally-defined recipient) must qualify for the Disability Tax Credit. The beneficiary must not be older than 59 years and needs to be a Canadian resident.

Contributions to an RDSP are not tax-deductible, but the money in the plan grows tax-free. Only the recipient will pay taxes on the growth of the money they withdraw from the plan. The government of Canada also offers special savings incentives, like grants and bonds, to help the money in the RDSP grow. When you put funds into an RDSP, the government will also contribute in the form of a Canada Disability Savings Grant.

The amount depends on your contribution level and your family circumstances. The government provides more help for families with modest income by adding extra funds to the Canada Disability Savings Grant and by providing further assistance in the form of a Canada Disability Savings Bond.

· There are also a number of locked-in plans, registered pension plans and numerous other retirement savings vehicles that may be available at your workplace. Each one of these has a set of tax advantages and a subsequent cost in terms of regulations.

Non-registered financial plans

Non-registered accounts are the accounts you set up with a financial institution where you do not enter into a special agreement with CRA to get tax sheltering. Non-registered accounts tax the capital gains (profit) generated in that account, at 50 per cent of the account holder's top marginal tax rate. As well, growth in the form of interest, dividends and distributions are taxed at rates lower than income tax rates.

Investment accounts have no limits on contributing, timelines for withdrawing or deadlines. You are free to invest in what you choose, how you choose it and when. In summary, you do not receive any immediate tax breaks, but you are taxed at lower than your income tax rate, which is the RRSP withdrawal rate.

Informed confidence

Investing is work and requires overcoming many psychological and material obstacles. I often say that the work of investing is *self-control*. Emotional management is rewarded with the long-term satisfaction of having achieved financial success. This happens when you set up your strategy, make your choices, understand the reasons why you have made these choices and then commit to seeing it through.

What fees are fair?

WE'VE ALREADY TALKED about the **internal fees** on a mutual fund (MERs) and the **commissions** you might pay. In addition, when you open a registered account, the institution will typically charge you a **trustee fee** because they have to register with the CRA and then report on your account.

With broker dealers (investment firms), where you are buying and selling stocks and bonds, you will either pay commissions on the transactions that occur, or you will pay an **annual fee** that is charged either monthly or quarterly.

Sometimes these fees are not advantageous for you. For instance, paying commissions may be better for you if you are going to just hold on to what you have for the next ten years and do not require selling or buying advice (not a situation I see that often or would recommend). If you don't hear from your advisor and don't use their advice at all, then why pay for it?

Fees for full service can be very good value. With a professional to watch your accounts and provide financial planning, investment strategy and tax planning, you are truly receiving full service. The financial rewards of avoiding mistakes, unnecessary taxes and poor timing in buying or selling can more than pay for the fees. Conversely, we often see investment accounts in which it appears that advisors are charging fees but not providing service or adequate oversight of the portfolio. It's up to you to negotiate what you want the relationship to look like, and what that advisor is set up to deliver or chooses to give you, before you decide whether that fee structure is appropriate and has value for you.

This process may seem long and arduous, but it protects you from the insanity that is often perpetuated by well-meaning friends and the media. The market goes up and down all day, all week and all year, for every decade it has been in existence. Throughout time, well diversified, intelligently chosen portfolios have gone up after they have gone down. And they went up more than down. There are exceptions, and if there weren't it wouldn't be a fair market place. Focus on increasing your knowledge so that you can expand your capacity for managing your emotions during the upheavals and you are more likely to be rewarded with the financial success you have always wanted.

STEP FOUR TO-DO LIST:
Remember, you do not have to understand how to put a portfolio together or even look at the quality or composition of the individual holdings. This is for a professional to sweat over.

· You have your goals established from Step Three.
· You (and your financial advisor) set up an asset allocation structure for each of the goals, and therefore, each portfolio has a different structure.
· The advisor selects a wide mix of investments that go into each of the classes, in each of the portfolios. These selections are based on your ability to withstand volatility and the safety you need in terms of preservation of your capital.
· You agree on a fee structure that works for you and the advisor. You are now ready to determine how you are going to keep track of your progress.

10

——— STEP FIVE ———

HOW DO I
STAY ON TRACK?

////////////////////////

DECIDING HOW and when to review and monitor your financial plan is an essential and ongoing part of the wealth-building process, one that is often overlooked by advisors and investors.

We can't just write out our financial plan and then put it on the shelf for ten years, hoping it will all work out. Our life changes. We might be getting married or divorced, having kids or having kids move out, buying a business or selling a business. A lot can happen in a year, and our investment strategy may no longer match our goals.

So, how do we do keep track of our financial life? Each person is going to have different needs for monitoring, depending on the changeability of their life, their investments, their knowledge level and the number of advisors they have on their team. How often should you scrutinize your financial data? Whether it be cash flow, net worth or your investment statements, frequency is dictated by your personal preferences, time availability, stage of life and the complexity of your holdings. Like cash reserve, it is highly personal. I know we all like nice simple rules, but ownership and empowerment is all about making choices based on your own needs and preferences.

If you have a financial advisor, you may agree on a schedule where you meet once a quarter, every half year or even annually, if things are stable. You may have set criteria for checking in when there is a change in either direction. I think it's important for an advisor to alert a client about a new tax law or economic change that may affect them. And it is also important for a client to alert their advisor if there is a change that may affect risk tolerance, strategy or tax planning.

You may see your banker once every four months, your accountant twice a year and your estate lawyer only when there are material changes to your circumstances that will affect your legacy.

You may decide you want to take a very hands-on approach to monitoring things or a simplified, more detached approach. It is interesting to note that some very successful investors only check their statements once a year. It's the easiest way to avoid those psychological temptations that are triggered in the ups and downs. If you trust your advisor and get weirded out with volatility, you may simply choose to take a longer-term perspective in your tracking plan.

Some people track trades on a daily basis, but personally I wouldn't recommend daily monitoring of investment accounts, unless you are training yourself to learn about volatility. If you're not careful, an overzealous, over-vigilant approach can actually put you back to sleep, because you're not focusing on the right things, and you can create stress and anxiety that is not necessary. Welcome to Fuss Factor activation. It's like your weight: if you stand on a scale seven times a day, you don't really know if you've lost weight. You become hyper-focused on what's going on that day. So, if you've gone up 15 or 16 ounces but lose sight of the fact that you've lost 55 pounds in the last year, you run the risk of self-sabotage and unnecessary anxiety. You don't see the forest for the trees.

The purpose of monitoring is to know when and if a decision needs to be made. You want to know whether you are on track to achieve your objectives or veering off course. Some people will check their bank balances on a daily basis, some monthly. When people are at the wealth-accumulation stage, they may have to look at their cash flow on a daily basis. Maybe they will even check in hourly, if they are on a one-to-three-month tracking program to get a handle on their flow.

Most people actually don't know how to read their investment or bank statements. The statements you receive from your broker dealer (investment firm), if you have a stock and bond account, are legally mandated by iiroc (our national investment industry authority) to track the flow of every penny in your account. This is to ensure transparency of transactions. You will be able to see everything that has happened in an account, but you will not get a good picture of your returns or the long-term view from these monthly statements.

To accurately gauge your progress, you will need specially prepared quarterly or biannual reports that are specifically designed to provide information like whether you are up or down, how much you paid in fees in that period, how your portfolio measures up against the benchmarks and why certain buys and sells occurred. You can also use something like an Excel spreadsheet or an account book or an online tracking program to watch the movement of the value of your accounts if your advisor doesn't provide them (although they should—and the reports should be structured in a way that you understand).

Ultimately, at the root of all reporting methods lies the questions "Am I getting there, or aren't I?" and "Am I up, or am I down?" A good monitoring process is about finding a way to check whether we're on the right path to get where we want to go. We need the strength to stick to what we set out to do. We need the wisdom to know when a change needs to be made. We want to know whether we have to change course now so that we can reach our goals or whether we actually have to change the goals themselves.

In my experience, it takes about three years for a woman to go from having no ownership about her finances to feeling that she understands her own situation and the language of her financial plan. Our life, our status, career and knowledge—as well as our wealth—all exist along a continuum. Our tracking and evaluation process is no different.

We go through a process of making choices about how we want to receive information about our finances and how we can manage the professionals in our life by asking questions and getting the answers we need, instead of placating them or being bossed around. When we stay on track, we emerge with a sense of empowerment about our whole financial plan, the choices we've made and the actions that are necessary to achieve our dreams.

STEP FIVE TO-DO LIST:
- Talk to your advisor about how and when you will be reviewing your progress.
- Collect up your statements and circle the parts you don't understand. Get clarification.
- Choose the lines and the statements that you consider most valuable for tracking.
- Decide on a method for charting and evaluating the big picture, and input the values from your statements in that format on a predetermined schedule.

11

GUIDES AND HELPERS

////////////////////////

O**NE OF** the most beautiful *and* terrible things about becoming financially empowered is the necessity for assistance along the way. It is ironic that in order to become independent and truly self-sufficient, we need to have help, and we need to determine the roles and identities of our helpers. Many people avoid this whole set of tasks because it is so challenging.

The inherent contradiction of showing our vulnerability to someone so that we can get strong can trip up the bravest of women. Every time we show what we don't know, we expose ourselves. As a financial professional, I can tell you without question that I cannot manage the investment and financial planning needs of my clients without a team. No matter how knowledgeable, intelligent and experienced we are, we need the wisdom of others to make the best decisions. The theme of this whole section is that building a good relationship with professionals you like and respect is incredibly valuable.

In my case, I have a brilliant business partner whose brain operates on a different wavelength than mine. This ensures that all aspects of a situation are looked at from two completely diverse perspectives. Then we pull in a variety of other professionals for consultation about and collaboration with our clients. We may need the firm's librarian to research the cost basis of a long-held or inherited stock position. We may need to confer with a tax accountant specializing in German tax law or a family lawyer who can explain a section of a separation agreement. The list is endless.

This same collegial approach is necessary for each of us personally, as well. In many areas of your life you already do this. You may have a "beauty team" comprising your hair stylist colour specialist, nail esthetician, fitness trainer, dermatologist and maybe even a plastic surgeon! We seem to take this part of our lives very seriously. We trust ourselves to determine whether the haircut we got makes us look better or, God forbid, like our mothers. We will not put up with makeup that looks garish on us or clothing that doesn't suit us. We change salons when we are not happy with the service we receive, and we believe we have the right to look and feel good throughout the process while receiving their services.

For some reason, this same sense of authority isn't often experienced when it comes to our money and the helpers we need to manage it successfully. Why is this? I wonder if the impediments are both conscious and unconscious. Or maybe practical and psychological. I have seen a great deal of confusion among clients about which financial professional does what and even more confusion about what role they themselves should play. With my hairstylist, I know what her job is. By the time I have reached adulthood, I have built up enough experience with my hair that I am quite confident in knowing the job I need done for me and what my professional expects back from me. With an accountant or investment specialist, you may not be so sure.

This uncertainty can be well founded. It is very hard to separate the various roles and licences of professionals in the financial realm. After working in the U.S. as a financial advisor, it took me more than a year after I returned to Canada to figure out what all the acronyms meant and who did what. I became very aware of the complexity and contradictions and am very sympathetic to this confusion, as I've been confused too.

The other aspects of our discomfort are in the psychological realm. I often hear confessions from women that they are fearful of looking stupid. I get it—I'm pretty insecure about my wardrobe taste. I've learned that I'm naturally kind of dowdy and, frankly, have quite an appalling sense of colour. I've coped with these weaknesses through the years by always wearing black bottoms! The idea that I could stand in front of an audience and have the women thinking, "My God, what is she wearing?" for some reason worries me a lot. This is the area where I most need guidance and have the least confidence in my ability to hire the right people to help me. I understand the irony of needing support but not trusting myself to bring in the correct people and experiences. So, when you come to my book launch, I will probably be wearing a black skirt.

Emotionally, I think we want someone to rescue us from our own insecurities and weaknesses. We do need professional advice in all areas of our lives and this is where the real efficiencies in life management come in. A financial advisor I worked with once said, "Our clients need to know how to tell time, not how to build the watch." I loved that advice because it speaks to the client's role as one of oversight, not micromanagement. It makes sense.

HOW DO I BEGIN ASSEMBLING MY MONEY TEAM?

First, we do some of that internal work we have talked about before. We need to "own" our situation by taking stock of what we don't know. This isn't that difficult in practical terms, but for some reason it seems to create stress. I guess it's like my feelings when I walk into a clothes shop: I want to look absolutely fabulous and five pounds lighter, wear colours that take off ten years and the outfit to be on sale. But when it comes down to it, what I really want is for the salesperson to know this without me having to confess it. Sometimes I get lucky and hit exactly the right person, who takes me to a part of the store I would never have considered and begins pulling out perfect selections. But it's been about 12 years since that happened, so I have had to become more specific about explaining what I want.

With money, you start working out your helpers by looking at the three overarching goals you determined in your financial planning. I want to have $20,000 in cash reserve, take a year off to travel, retire at age 70, buy a home, or purchase a cottage. Just like it's better if I determine before entering a store that I want to pay no more than $500 for a suit and that it should be lined, in my colour palette (I carry one of these around after my friend Christine did my colours two years ago) and able to be packed up in a suitcase easily without wrinkling, I need to articulate to the salesperson that comfort really matters to me and I am not averse to a little tailoring to get it to fit properly. That at least puts me in greater control of the situation and increases the likelihood that I will get my needs met. So, with your priorities established, you can determine which of the helpers we talk about will fit you.

When I first started as a financial advisor in the U.S. for Smith Barney, I was put through eight hours of achievement and psychological testing. They had a hiring policy at the time that if they took you on, you needed to be someone who was worthy of the massive investment they would put into your success. I was also interviewed by no fewer than three managers and four branch employees. By the time they offered me employment, they were fairly certain that I had the personality and ability to succeed.

How is your securities licensed advisor paid?

SECURITIES LICENSED ADVISORS vary in terms of their compensation structures. Some work for fees, and others work on commission. This can raise some issues for clients.

When a firm pressures their advisors to achieve certain sales goals or risk termination, there is an inherent conflict: the advisor's desire to do what's right for the client and the competing desire to stay employed. These do not always line up.

There is also a problem when firms reward the sales of an internal product higher than a competitor's product. This impedes (as it is intended to) the objectivity of the recommendation. These issues plague the industry and can impede a person's trust that the advice they receive is actually in their best interest. When an advisor charges a fee rather than working on commission, it means that the advisor is not rewarded for *just* selling something. They become responsible for the outcome of their advice.

Commission works better when either the client has made a decision about a straight buy-and-hold transaction and simply needs it implemented or when a great deal of front end work is necessary for a recommendation (on certain complex insurance products, for example) and very little follow up is needed.

Then came the huge investment in my training. For four months, I was in courses to help me pass my securities exam, courses on best practices for portfolio management and additional training in ethics and codes of conduct. Once licensed, I was legally able to buy and sell securities under the watchful eye of the broker dealer. In Canada, I went through the same process again to become licensed to sell and buy securities here.

This is basic training, like someone fresh out of hairdressing school. Some salons have apprenticeship programs and the new staff member is watched over by managers or more experienced stylists. In other situations, a new graduate could just start snipping on a street corner.

Different financial firms have varying degrees of supervision standards for their advisors. You either want someone who is with a very strict firm known for its compliance record, or you want someone with at least five years' experience, who has experimented on everyone else and knows what they are doing. This is a good benchmark for every member of your financial team. But who do you need on your team now?

SECURITIES LICENSED ADVISORS

A **securities licensed advisor**, or full-service advisor, is one who is legally allowed to buy and sell individual stocks, bonds and other securities on your behalf.

They must be licensed by IIROC and have a relationship with a broker dealer. The broker dealer manages the training and reporting function and ensures that the advisor complies with securities laws. They are like a parent company overseeing the advisor. In our case, Raymond James is the broker dealer, even though we own Sophia Financial Group.

I believe people need a full-service advisor when they are at an asset level of about $250,000 or more. At that point, their financial situation has reached a certain level of complexity and would benefit from the more stringent licensing of the securities regulators and the ability to use a wider range of products (stocks, bonds, mutual funds, REITs). Mutual funds may no longer be the most efficient instrument for the bulk of their assets.

If you have much less than that to invest, you probably don't have the capacity to diversify your holdings enough to manage risk, so mutual funds may be the best place for your money, and you don't need a IIROC-licensed advisor for those.

Some financial advisors are licensed just to sell mutual funds and are referred to as MFDA (Mutual Fund Dealers Association of Canada) licensed. They specialize in the products their firm allows and are experienced at putting together mutual fund portfolios. They can work independently, within a firm or within a bank or credit union.

In a bank, if they can only sell that institution's house-managed mutual funds, they have the least amount of investment knowledge, but the belief is that they also can do the least amount of harm. Most of the time, bank-managed funds have reasonable management fees (MER), and the initial deposit requirements are also low. This can make them a great choice for beginning investors. My own children use the mutual funds of their respective banks, but they have my guidance and investment knowledge supporting them. That's not a bad combination. Mutual fund salespeople, regardless of where they work, are rewarded for selling these funds and are sometimes reluctant to refer you to an advisor who could analyze a wider range of options.

FINANCIAL PLANNERS

A good option for those starting out or who are going through significant life transitions is to hire a financial planner, and there are a few ways to do that. There are financial planners at banks that will work with you at a certain threshold or dollar amount of assets to be managed. They sometimes charge planning fees and sometimes don't. The quality of these plans is as varied as the qualifications and experience of the financial planners who create them. Regularly, people come into our offices hauling 60- or 70-page plans that have a ton of disclaimers and a myriad of charts and graphs and numbers in such small print and high volume that they create an instant yearning for unconsciousness. I used to read mutual fund prospectuses to help me fall asleep, and some of these plans could rival them in battling insomnia!

Financial planning should be a meaningful process. It should answer the questions that live in you and pose others that you hadn't thought of. Without life context, they are meaningless. Nor are they a panacea for what ails you. Just having a whopping big plan is in no way a guarantee that financial success is on the agenda, and I would advise you to be a careful consumer in this area.

The most common model for financial planners is one in which a written plan is formulated and the implementation of investment purchasing is done with the same person.

The advantage is that it is a one-stop shop. The person who now has a deep understanding of your situation can match appropriate products to the plan. Detractors believe that this arrangement can muddy the objectivity of the planner, because ultimately they are rewarded by making a commission on the sale of a product. Again, how someone is compensated does shape their behaviour, but there is a wide variety of ethical standards and beliefs about how this actually plays out.

There is also a model for fee-only financial planning, where you get only the advice. Fee-only financial planners are paid by the hour or by project. These fees can range from $2,500 to $5,000 per plan, or $100 to $300 an hour, depending on the complexity of the financial plan and the amount of time spent with the client. There is often a strong emphasis on personal financial education with many of the best planners. But there is also the risk that you will end up with a honking big plan and no real understanding of how to implement it. I have seen various forms of this.

MONEY COACHES

At various times in your life, there may be a role for a **money coach**. These professionals (hopefully with their financial planning designations) will help you clarify goals, identify blocks to economic success and create a system to help you get out of debt and start allocating monies to short-, medium- and long-term goals. The coaching model works beautifully when there is a personal impediment to be tackled that goes deeper than just dollars and cents. A coach is helpful when you are very new to the money world, have long-standing debt issues, feel powerless or are simply in need of one-on-one mentorship from an educated professional.

Your choice to make

Regulatory supervision, education level and experience are very, very important when choosing an advisor. But this is just the baseline. What is most important is that you feel well served. This is the area where your intuition should be on full alert.

I believe that making financial decisions is a "head game," that portfolio decisions should be made rationally, factually, using all existing data to make the best possible choices. But I don't believe this is the best way to choose an advisor. If you feel in any way disrespected, condescended to, patronized, ashamed or uncomfortable with your advisor, fire them! But, before you do, have a clarifying conversation. Use language like "When I ask you a question, I would prefer if you answered in sentences. I don't understand the graphs you always point at." Or "When I don't understand something you say, simply raising your voice and using the same words doesn't help." Or "Hello.

Hello! I'm over here! This is my investment portfolio, not my husband's, and I would like you to address me." You get to practise using your voice to ask for what you want. A long, drawn-out discussion may not be necessary, but having a dialogue about what you do or don't want in the relationship is. This may also include outlining the method and frequency of contact or your reporting preferences.

In most situations, it's better to give your advisor the opportunity to correct their behaviour. For the most part, they probably want you to understand what they are saying. I believe that most of the financial advisors I know would rather be liked and appreciated than fired. But not all of them are able, or care enough, to alter their behaviour.

So, those were the financial advisory roles in a nutshell: advisors who sell only mutual funds and the IIROC-licensed advisors who also can advise on all products tied to the equity and debt market. There are financial planners who sell product and those who just do planning.

HELP WITH DEBT

Most of us juggle some debt, and not all of it is bad. There can be good, productive reasons for borrowing money. But if your debt is growing despite your intention to shrink it, or if it has grown so large that it dwarfs your income and ability to repay it, then you know it has become a problem.

Severe debt is one of the most stressful conditions a person can face, causing anxiety, shame and panic. This can exacerbate the money problem, because if your feelings are running out of control, you can't use them to guide you, and clear guidance is absolutely essential.

If you find yourself in this type of situation, you might benefit from seeing an **insolvency specialist** or **trustee**. These professionals are licensed by the federal government agency Industry Canada to administer legislative options for dealing

Borrowing isn't always bad

THERE ARE MANY areas where borrowing is a good strategy. I still like to see people looking at home ownership if possible. This is a great way to control your monthly shelter expense in the long term. So, a mortgage can be a very sound option if you can't pay for a whole house outright (like the majority of us). Also, money for retraining, career advice and higher education is an investment that can lead to a greater payoff, and one where you bear the lion's share of control of the outcome. Being the author of your own destiny and investing in yourself is a very exciting way to manage a life and an appropriate place to spend money.

I am also a big believer in investing in a business. The greatest female income earners in this country own their own companies. I come from four generations of entrepreneurs. When my parents needed to increase their income, they simply increased their value to the community by starting another business. I learned to scan for business opportunities on a daily basis. Dinner conversation revolved around different business possibilities. It was a sport. And this is from a very working-class background. All of these are sensible ways to increase your value, and debt can enable you to do that. You know how much you can handle, and if you don't, you can get advice.

with serious or long-standing debt issues. They hold the special designation of Chartered Insolvency and Restructuring Specialist, which means that they are overseen by regulatory bodies and must meet expectations of conduct and integrity. They also have to fulfill requirements for ongoing professional development. These specialists are legally accountable to all stakeholders in the situation—the debtor, the creditors and the court.

This is different from the credit counselling, debt management and debt settlement businesses you see regularly advertised as non-profits. There are some very good ones out there, but they have no regulatory oversight. The other drawback to using these companies is that creditors are not legally required to cooperate with them, as when a trustee is involved. Because they can only work with creditors that choose to participate in their programs, they may be unable to help you with some, or all, of your debt problem, depending on whom you owe money to. This can leave you with a very tangled knot that is even harder to unravel.

With a licensed trustee or insolvency specialist, all creditors are drawn in by law and dealt with. If you fear you might be in financial trouble, you can get a free assessment that looks at the debt situation and its relationship to assets and income levels. It's the trustee's job to educate you on the various options available. They may even make a referral to a credit-counselling agency or talk to you about the benefits and disadvantages of bankruptcy or the consumer proposal process.

There are specialists in both consumer and corporate debt. The insolvency (debt) specialist is compensated in a regulated and consistent manner across Canada. The fees are typically paid to the specialist as a percentage of the money distributed to creditors, but there may be some other costs involved that you will be informed of.

When someone goes through bankruptcy or a consumer proposal process, the government mandates that they receive just two financial counselling sessions. As you can imagine, this leaves a lot to be dealt with. Although the process may resolve your most serious debt headache, the underlying behaviours, thought processes and conditions that brought you to that place may not get addressed, and very few people seek out additional counselling.

Most debt situations arise from a series of decisions and long-standing habits as well as emotional needs that may go unaddressed for a whole lifetime. A debt crisis is an opportunity to bring these into the light. It might take a whole well-being program as well as financial education to resolve it permanently.

PERSONAL SUPPORT

We've already discussed the role of emotions and the large part they play in managing your financial life. They come into play whether you want them to or not, when your values are being threatened or supported or when some message you have believed in your whole life gets activated and brought to the surface.

They come in during particularly stressful life transitions like marriage, divorce, death or selling a business. They can assist us by guiding us towards a path that feels good and right and, hopefully, away from those things that are not in alignment with our values and goals.

However, when a woman's mental state is clouded by too much emotion, she is not in a great place to make life-affecting decisions.

So, what do you do if you find yourself in a state of emotional activation? The advisor you need to call on would be **a mental health professional** with either a master's or doctoral degree, who is registered by a licence-granting governing body. This could be a **social worker, psychologist, registered clinical counsellor, grief therapist** or **psychiatrist** (especially if there is a medical condition associated with your emotional distress).

You would look for someone with whom you feel a strong sense of rapport and respect. Grief counsellor Sony Baron advises that a woman should feel some difference in her mental state by the fourth visit to a therapist, and if she doesn't, she should question the process and perhaps look for another practitioner.

Typically, mental health professionals charge by the hour, depending on their geographic location, experience level and educational background. I will often recommend that a woman get counselling before making any financial decisions if it looks like emotions are running strong and she would benefit from emotional support. We need to know that we are in full control and command of our faculties before making what can be life-changing, irrevocable decisions.

CAREER MANAGEMENT

We have talked about the importance of work to financial success. Unless you are independently wealthy, you will need to figure out the best way to exchange your talents, education and abilities for money. And naturally, you will want to make sure that you are getting the highest compensation possible in this exchange.

For most women, managing a career requires active involvement. With today's increasingly fluid workforce, it's not enough just to land a job and stick with it for life—you need to optimize your abilities all along your own personal career path.

A woman may benefit from the support of a **career advisor** when she graduates, when she transitions back to work after parental leave or after losing a job. She may need to find out what career options exist in her field, learn how to negotiate a salary and benefits package, increase her value in the job market and figure out how best to leverage a practical talent or passion. There are a myriad of workplace scenarios where an outside opinion can be very valuable and, indeed, lead to a better financial life.

As I previously stressed, one of the best places a person can invest their money is in themselves. (But remember, we're not talking about those job-interview shoes.)

An excellent career advisor can lead to financial returns many times over. High-calibre career testing, interpretation and coaching can help avoid years of unsatisfactory or inappropriate job placement. And figuring out how to make more money for working the same number of hours (increasing the exchange value of your worth) is a fabulous investment. I regularly advise women to set aside money for this advice.

To assess whether a particular career advisor is a good fit, you may want to ask about their methods and approach, the testing methods they employ, their training and education (preferably at least a master's degree, if possible) and the target clients and situations they specialize in. There are many styles and approaches, and you should ask the questions you want answered about their process. You will want to clarify what you need help with and match it with the advisor's area of expertise. And above all, you should have a sense that you are in good hands with this person.

Most career professionals are compensated with hourly fees. Expect rates to be higher for those who are more experienced and those who work with management-level workers and professionals. You may get a package rate, or you may even have a retainer kind of relationship for a specified time period, such as after a job loss. The basic foundation of self-determination is creating optimal income for satisfying work. It is worth the outlay needed to achieve that goal.

BANKS AND CREDIT UNIONS

Once you have income and work issues sorted out, you will want to look at your choice of **primary financial institution**. In fact, the single most important financial relationship that most Canadians develop is with a **bank** or **credit union** (I will use the word bank from here on to mean both). Our economic environment is largely dominated by the conduct and practices of our biggest financial institutions.

In every one of our workshops, we see women get riled up on the topic of banks. Almost everyone in the room has at one time or another felt spurned by their financial institution. They tell stories of humiliation, condescension and abandonment.

Or perhaps you've never given your choice of bank much consideration. Maybe it happened to be the nearest one to your home many years ago, and you haven't given it a second thought since. You might have barely even spoken to anyone there, especially if you usually use the ATM and their website to do your banking.

It doesn't have to be that way. Banks want a relationship with you—that part is easy. But you also have a role to play in ensuring that the relationship works, and there are strategies you can use to get your needs met.

The first step to losing your intimidation is to develop an understanding of how banks work.

It's important to recognize that even with their philanthropic and social missions, the bank must make money. They have shareholders and a board of directors, and they make no statements to suggest that they are a charity. Nor should they. They are primarily holders and protectors of capital. We count on them to not lose our money after we deposit it. We also expect them to loan us money.

Most institutions have your accounts sitting in a portfolio overseen by a personal **account manager**. Finding and connecting with that person isn't always straightforward. Last week, I needed to speak to my banker by phone. It turns out that mine had gone on some kind of leave, so I waded through six levels of choices on the customer service line to get the name and number of my new person. Then it took two days for us to connect. This is my fourth account manager in seven years. It is a constant lament from our clients that it is impossible to have a relationship when everyone keeps moving. And it is annoying. But I am advising you to do what I just did. Grin and bear it. For your own sake, you need to make a personal connection with your banker.

Borrowing from the bank

BANKS ARE THE primary supplier of credit for most Canadians. And as you know from our previous sidebar about good and bad debt on pages 89 to 90, credit can be a double-edged sword.

Most of us need credit cards. They help us make plane reservations, book hotels and make purchases online. They can be a great convenience but are not intended to be a long-term lending strategy. Another common loan is a credit line, often using our homes as collateral. Collateral is property or goods that are used to secure a loan. They can be liquidated to cover the bank's loss if you are unable to pay the debt back. Again, a credit line can have useful applications. Credit lines are handy when you want to start a business and need seed capital. The rates of interest are often lower than for a traditional business loan, and there is little documentation necessary to get access to funds. However, unlike the application for a business loan where a full business case needs to be made, a credit line is established on ability to repay and the asset value backing it. The ease of obtaining this credit is also its downside.

I hear two things quite regularly that concern me. The first issue is that if you're borrowing money to start a business, you might be able to fund it without ever putting a business plan in place. Using credit for a poorly thought out business or one that is doomed to fail is obviously a bad financial decision.

The second is that some people think that the amount the bank loans you is a form of endorsement that you can safely go out and spend that amount. Remember, that nice young person behind the counter (or on the phone) is rewarded for extending credit to you. If you go into the back staff rooms of your neighbourhood banks, you will see target tracking of each employee. They are rewarded for selling you extra credit. They win trips, receive bonuses and even earn Starbucks gift cards. They are not wise, all-knowing specialists who see into the window of your soul to determine your worthiness—they are pressured employees who want to keep their jobs. You are the one who knows your personal circumstances thoroughly enough to determine if that is too much credit risk for you to take on.

Many of us have lost sight of what is a liability and what is an asset. I have recently seen situations where young people put their credit line capacity in the asset column of their net worth statement. How's that for changing times? We have become a "pay it off" not "save up for" society and this is reflected in our ever-increasing debt levels.

She or he will be invaluable if you need help with an account problem or credit for a start up, or if you find something you don't understand on your monthly statement. It is worth the time and energy to connect with them.

A common misconception many women have is that "diversification by institution"—using multiple banks—is a sound risk management principle. It isn't. It can increase the complexity of management, and you can more easily lose track of what is going on in your financial life. I liken it to the idea of having three nannies to decrease the chance that one might be abusive. It makes no sense at all when you think about it. You put your child at more, not less, risk. So, it's far better to increase your value with the bank you work with. This is what gets you better rates and more personal service.

Banks control how money moves in this world, so getting a firm handle on a banking relationship will serve you well.

MORTGAGE SPECIALISTS

At some point, you may want a member on your team who can help you to buy a house.

A **mortgage specialist** who works at your bank can play a valuable role in the process. She can look at the relationship of your other bank-held assets and make knowledgeable recommendations about how much you can afford, how much the bank will loan you and the various mortgage options. A bank mortgage specialist can also oversee your overall credit strategy, linking your mortgage with other lending options within that bank.

When I first moved back to Canada, I was introduced to a mortgage specialist at a bank. Not only did she educate me on the various options; she referred us to a terrific realtor and connected me to my first fantastic banker, who oversaw the capable transfer of our accounts from the U.S. She became a stellar example of banking excellence on behalf of her institution.

Later I found out that she had the foresight to anticipate our need for business credit and set up a lending structure for us that has since been incredibly beneficial. A mortgage is a very profitable product for a bank and increases your value to them.

However, there are advantages to going with an **independent mortgage broker**. Because they are not employees of a particular institution, they can provide a more objective and unbiased overview of pricing and options in the marketplace.

A mortgage broker can work with all the banks and credit unions and has a network of alternative lenders for special circumstances. She is paid a finder's fee by a lender when a deal closes, and these fees (as with bankruptcy trustees) are standardized across the industry, so there is no incentive to choose one lender over another.

Because mortgage brokers are licensed and regulated, they must meet industry suitability and educational requirements. In the event of a complaint against a mortgage broker, FICOM (Financial Institutions Commission) will investigate and impose disciplinary actions if needed. It's also a good idea to check to see if the broker holds an AMP (Accredited Mortgage Professional) designation. This ensures that they have completed educational requirements and continue to upgrade their knowledge by completing ongoing annual educational courses.

Regardless of your choice of mortgage specialist or broker, it is important to be working with someone who returns your calls and emails promptly and who you connect with personally. Buying a home can be very stressful, and the process can move very quickly, so you want to work with someone you know, like and trust.

ACCOUNTANTS AND BOOKKEEPERS

If you hate Excel spreadsheets and calculators make you sick to your stomach, it makes sense to deal with them as little as possible.

Fortunately, the job of keeping track of your numbers and filling in those dreaded forms can be sub-contracted. You can still be financially empowered, and in fact may be more so, when you farm out the jobs you hate so that you can concentrate on your own "higher order" decision-making.

You need an **accountant** if your personal taxes are complicated or if there has been a significant change in your financial life, such as managing the estate of a family member. They are also helpful during the sale or purchase of a large asset or if you're making any decision that has tax implications.

If you run a business, your accountant can be a key player in your advisory team. They can help you with issues ranging from cash flow analysis to determining profitability models to helping you make well-thought-out capital purchasing decisions. Your accountant can help you make decisions about your business salary and assist you in preparing end-of-year financial statements and tax returns. They can also advise you on how to pay the least amount of tax.

Professional accountants have three main designations in Canada: CA (**Chartered Accountant**), CGA (**Certified General Accountant**) and CMA (**Certified Management Accountant**). While most often CMA's focus more on internal business accounting, the business services offered by professional accountants vary more based on the personal preference and style rather than subject matter. To get an accounting designation requires four to eight years of post-secondary education and successful completion of rigorous professional courses and exams. An accountant is required to complete a prescribed number of courses of continuing education each year. Almost without exception, accountants charge an hourly rate. A good accountant helps you feel that your financial and tax affairs are well organized, up to date and set up to maximize your personal financial well-being.

Sometimes **bookkeepers** will call themselves accountants. A bookkeeper requires no licensing but will often have a diploma or undergraduate degree that enables them to do data entry and basic accounting and to record banking, sales and other transactions. They can complete a company's books before they are sent to the accountant for year-end financial statement and tax return preparation. This enables the CA to use their time for higher level tax and strategic business planning decisions.

Bookkeepers are not just for businesses. If you are one of those people who "hates numbers," but you want to manage your personal finances responsibly, hiring a bookkeeper may be the answer.

LAWYERS

At some point in your lifetime, you will need a **lawyer**. There are several situations in which this need may arise.

I would like to talk about the thorniest one first. The area of family law and mediation is often misunderstood. It has been traditionally used to resolve conflict using legal channels in combative situations, but lawyers can also be useful—and maybe even essential—in pre-empting the likelihood of conflict down the line or minimizing its impact.

Whenever you are entering into or leaving a spousal relationship, having a child with someone or deciding to live with a partner, you need to chat with a family lawyer. This isn't done to start a fight; it's done to ensure that you understand the legal constructs you are signing up for and going to be subject to.

You may also require a **mediator** at some point in your family life. They can help you find solutions by creating and holding a safe place for a conversation to happen. This can be invaluable in enabling people to move beyond a place of "stuckness." They can facilitate resolution of a dispute or create ideas and new options for solving a problem. I have watched some amazing breakthroughs occur when the people involved are supported to hear and be heard. Anything that resolves conflict is good for you financially. Conflict is expensive, but not dealing with it is more so.

Another lawyer that you will need on your team is an **estate specialist**. There is a big difference between an **estate lawyer**, also known as a wills and estate lawyer, and an **estate planning lawyer**. An estate lawyer will act as executor, or on behalf of an executor, to assist in the winding up of the estate of a deceased person. An estate planning lawyer is able to assist in the planning of personal financial and legal affairs in the event of disability or death.

Because we usually don't know when these inevitable life events will happen, and because failure to adequately plan can have serious, permanent and undesired consequences, estate planning is one of the first things a woman needs to have in place to protect herself on her financial journey.

Choosing a competent lawyer can be a bit tricky. Like doctors, there are many variations in defining what constitutes "a good one." One person likes a brusque manner, and the other wants a more collaborative approach. Some rookie lawyers are crackerjacks, and some who have been practising for thirty years are incompetent. Can your friend refer you? Maybe. But I think it's hard for a layperson to judge competence. Lawyers are very good at knowing the capabilities of other lawyers and may be good sources for referrals, as are other professionals who regularly deal with lawyers.

You want to make sure you feel a sense of trust, connection and intelligence when you are with them, and that they convey respect and attention. A good lawyer is someone who uses their legal knowledge to support your values and to achieve your objectives using the structures of the law. Technical competency is one aspect, but relationship and an understanding of you is just as important.

FRIENDS AND SUPPORT GROUPS

Last but not least, you need your *friends*. But in the context of this discussion about money, it's a certain kind of friend that you need. The kind of friend you can talk to about your kids or husband with is different from the kind of friend you can discuss money with.

I love women. I think we are going to save the planet. But I'm also aware of some of our shadows, and money is often in the darkest part of our psychological closet. I have watched women talk about their pubic hair, hot flashes and lack of orgasms with greater ease than their cash flow or asset allocation strategy.

I was recently out with a new friend who was excitedly reporting on her purchase of a new condo. I asked what price she paid for it. She just looked at me. Really stared. I noticed her discomfort and explained that it was the kind of thing I talked about every day. She did finally tell me the price, but I found her reluctance interesting. After all, it's almost public information, and not all that personal, is it? Nevertheless, I'm thinking that may be the last coffee she asks me out for.

There are many different **groups** a woman can join to further her journey with money. Sometimes I think it's even easier to form money connections with people with whom we don't have pre-existing relationships. It can seem easier to enter into intimate financial discussions with people we don't know all that well.

There are various ways to do this. For instance, at the Sophia Wealth Academy, **money groups** seem to form organically from rows of participants or haphazardly by people who sit together at lunch. Many of these groups have been meeting now for years. They have overcome debt together, conquered their RRSPS and negotiated salaries. The stories are wonderful.

There are also several **financial book clubs** that have originated from Wealth Academy. I love these clubs. They increase knowledge and then ground the information in personal experience. You can go far using that kind of model. The great thing about books is that the information and perspective is more enduring than in magazines and newspapers, which tend to be more short-sighted, leading you to miss important long-term principles.

There are also **investing clubs**, but these have mostly fallen by the wayside since I was a member of one in the nineties. Back then, the economy was growing so fast, you could be dumb as a stump and still make money in the stock market.

These groups don't have to be exclusively female in their membership. Including men can be very helpful, as long as they don't dominate the conversation or in any way impede women members' ability to open up and talk, which is pretty common in mixed groups when finances comes up. However, I must say that men do provide a different angle that can be illuminating for women. They can also speed up processes and help prevent Fuss Factor activation. Recently, I had a discussion about a difficult business issue I was facing with a long-time male friend. After I told him the story, he responded with the advice: "Armour yourself, ask for what you want, engineer it, then forget 'em if they can't take it." I just looked at him. It was great advice, and I can't think of a single woman friend who would have offered it so succinctly.

The paradigm I work with is: "We are stronger together than apart." A woman's ultimate ability to manage a complex life will arise from the efficiencies she builds in her network and advisory team. This means letting go of some of the details, surrendering some controls. It may also mean putting yourself in the path of some criticism or even career risk. It may also mean you have time to do yoga, feed the hungry and drink wine on Fridays with your friends. It means becoming interdependent in the name of asserting total independence. You intuitively know this and experience it in other areas of your life already.

I work with specialists in every one of these areas, and I benefit from their skills and support both professionally and personally. My capacity increases with assistance, and my sense of satisfaction increases when I can concentrate on the skills and abilities that make me happy and in which I excel. So will yours.

12

STAGES OF LIFE

///////////////////////

OUR LIFE journey takes us through many developmental stages and milestones.

There are years when we are accumulating assets, setting and working towards goals, spending time and money on others, having money spent on us, saving and spending. We go to school, graduate, go again; we get married, unmarried; we have children, children leave; we have times of illness and health.

Each of these phases has a price tag. And then there are the personal choices and decisions we make at every stage. Each of these has a personal consequence along with the related financial challenges and opportunities.

CHILDHOOD

One day when my son was about 11, I brought him with me to make a deposit after hours at our local bank. He and I were standing at the machine, and he watched me take cash and a couple of cheques from my wallet and insert them into the envelope and then into the machine. I looked over at him and his mouth was gaping open. I asked him what was the matter. He said to me incredulously, "You have to put money in those machines too?"

There is a lot written about raising money-smart kids and teaching children how to take responsibility for money. There are books and lectures and online platforms about this. It's not that complicated. But don't just assume they understand what is going on around them. They are forming their own pictures of reality from the clues that they see.

In our family, we were very talkative about money. The dinner table was a place where discussion about business and the stock market and taxes and the economy regularly took place. We thought our kids would just naturally understand certain basic principles of money management because of it. We were wrong. So, the first principle of raising a child who is financially competent is not to assume.

I often hear parents say, "You should know better than that." How should they? Explain the whole story of your financial transactions, including the things you think they already know. I'm not talking about lecturing. I'm talking about the kind of commentary that informs and explains. Technology may have made life more convenient for us, but the downside is that many of the cause-and-effect relationships in our transactions are masked, and it is actually more difficult now than ever to expose reality. We go off to work, so children do not actually see us work. We transfer money electronically rather than place the cash in our kids' hands, and we bank online and use machines that do not reveal the full story.

The second principle is to model the kind of behaviour you want your children to emulate. If you are whacked-out on credit, you cannot expect them to be fiscally prudent. If you have compensatory spending habits, they will not know the meaning of a dollar. They are not always listening but they *are* watching. Constantly. The best thing you can do is to be financially empowered and economically responsible yourself. Simple but not always easy.

ADOLESCENCE

I'm often asked to speak to teenagers in high schools about the stock market. Because I'm also a child development specialist, I tell them that for 16- or 17-year-olds, trying to understand stocks or bonds is not a developmentally appropriate use of their time and energy.

I am not impressed with stock-picking contests for kids who have never even opened a bank account and may never own a real stock. What are we teaching them, and why? As you saw from our financial planning steps, even the people who have a plan don't generally do their own stock picking. It's not a key financial skill by any means.

I think these attempts at money curriculums are a response to the idea that we should be teaching our kids basic financial skills, but they may not focus on the ones that are most important.

I believe an adolescent needs to learn about how credit and debit cards work; how to find satisfying, well-paid work; the reality of taxes; what banks do; and how to manage cash flow. Teens need to understand what debt is, how surplus is created and, most importantly, how to negotiate for what they want and need. These first tasks are very basic but are critical financial survival skills.

YOUNG ADULTHOOD

Last year, I was on a panel of professionals speaking with a group of young women from a local university business faculty. We were talking about money and power and paying attention. The facilitator kept encouraging the participants to tweet about the day and let the world know what was going on in our session.

Frankly, I found this annoying. We were trying to have a relevant and engaging discussion, and half the heads in the room were down, looking into their laps, thumbs frenzied. I asked them to put their devices away and to be present with us, to be here in the room, rather than *talking* about being here. My hypothesis is that much of the stress experienced by our young people stems from the fact that they are trying to be multi-taskers at an early age, and they are encouraged to be very proud of this ability (or imagined ability).

Many of my peers are going to ashrams and learning meditation techniques to learn to be "awake in this moment," because we recognize its importance for creative thinking and problem solving, as well as maintaining a peaceful mind. Many of the young people I interact with are not ever really present. Their bodies are present, but their minds are somewhere else.

Young women are also under incredible pressure to perform well in school, be sexy and beautiful, and save the planet in their spare time. They are a very stressed-out generation because of the many conflicting messages they are getting from media, their social world and their parents.

The financial tasks during this period are to get work or, more accurately, to begin the "work experiment," because in practise, they may need to go through several jobs before they figure out what they excel at and are happy with. They must learn to negotiate for what they want and don't want, to manage a bank account and to have positive cash flow. This should be done before any partnering or mothering is put on the table.

PARTNERING AND UN-PARTNERING

The advice to young women to find a career they love before starting a family has huge implications. It speaks to the importance of establishing a high level of independence, mentally and economically. When a woman feels she can make her own way and that she is financially self-sufficient, she is able to negotiate family issues with that knowledge supporting her. It changes those conversations because it changes the foundation you stand on when you have them.

I think that a woman's biggest impediment to a balanced life is the feeling that she has limited choices or that to be happy means being in a relationship at all costs, even if it requires a sacrifice of power. These misguided ideas are hurting us. To be financially empowered, you want to have your career on the right track.

These are also the years when people make decisions about marriage or living common-law and often face their first separations. Talking about money is still seen as somehow scheming and risky. And as we have spoken about earlier, many young women are under the impression that things are all going to magically work out. They hold the idea that they will be professionally successful, stay at home and look after their charming and healthy children, be supported by a better wage earner, and that this will all happen effortlessly while they maintain their dignity, autonomy and status. I remember my own mother getting so frustrated with me and my friends when we were in our late twenties. She felt we were not as vigilant as we needed to be, because the gains of the feminist movement were not as secure as we thought. She was right, and I find myself just as frustrated thirty years later.

Because of our strong need for connection, women will often consciously or unconsciously sacrifice personal autonomy and their own needs to preserve a relationship. We may want to deny it, but I see it every day. This is one of the big battlefields of financial empowerment. If we continually choose caring for others and connection before the fulfillment of our own mission and needs, there will continue to be significant consequences that are mostly not in our favour.

How many women do you know who actually negotiated a financial agreement before they got married or partnered? Not many.

To remain in the driver's seat of your own life, it's essential to understand the legal consequences of the life choices you are making. This knowledge may change how you structure the ownership of property, your will and estate plan (we'll get to that later) and even the very idea of who stays home with the children.

Romance doesn't have to mean remaining ignorant, although I do fear that women can perhaps be more misty-eyed than they care to admit. As the laws are changing in Canada to reflect new ideas of what constitutes family and the concept of fairness, it behooves even the most idealistic couple to look at what these laws mean to them.

For instance, as of March 2013 in British Columbia, the laws of property changed significantly in co-habitation and spousal relationships. Every person should know what their net worth is *before* they say "I do" or "Let's have a baby!" or even "Let's live together." Instead of the equal division of family property, you are now able to walk away with what you came into the relationship with, including inherited assets. You not only need to know your net worth, but your spouse or partner's as well. And not only do you have to fully understand your situation and that of your spouse-to-be; you will actually have to look at this together.

I know this brings up conflicting feelings and maybe even a bit of panic for many women. Do you want me to tell you more stories? Stories of women in their fifties being left penniless by their husbands? Or how about the heiress with $13 million who didn't want to tell her fiancé she was rich? Or I can tell you about the woman who had $80,000 in carefully concealed credit card debt or the teacher who had not disclosed to her live-in lover about her two former bankruptcies? (That'll be fun when she goes to do her mortgage application with Romeo.) Honestly, I get sad and sometimes very frustrated with these behaviours. Money matters, and you know it, or you wouldn't have the emotional resistance to discussing it with your partner.

This money conversation with a new partner is a great opportunity to bring up your assumptions about parenting roles too. Staying home to raise children is an economically disadvantageous choice of mammoth proportions, and it would be great if it were at least put on the table while the romantic collateral is high. You will never be in a better position to discuss thorny issues than before you actually make the decision to partner.

We are beyond the era of our mothers' teen years' warnings: "Why would he buy the cow when he can get the milk for free?" Today, the question is: "Why would you ever take on someone else's financial history without a conversation?"

I am in favour of doing a net worth statement and having a deep, soulful discussion about the financial life you want to have before you make any co-habitation decisions.

As a financial advisor, I often ask women how much their fiancé makes, what his pension looks like and whether he has debt. Most don't know, and many answer, "I would never ask him that!" But when you start living together, you are in a different ball game, and knowing the rules is helpful.

This avoidance of reality is not limited to the young. I recently spoke with a 62-year-old woman who was getting married for the first time. I was happy that she was so excited. Then she let it slip that he was $100,000 in debt. I asked her if she fully realized that she could be taking on 50 per cent of his debt. She did not want to talk about it. I offered to help her with the conversation so that they could dialogue about what it would mean to them in a non-confrontational and supported environment. She was very worried that he would think she didn't trust him and therefore not marry her. She didn't have the conversation, and I haven't heard from her since.

I spoke to a woman in her forties a few months ago who was cashing in her stock options and was going to get a payout of about $26 million. She was about to marry a younger man whom she had met while he was power washing her roof. He made about $40,000 a year. She asked for investment advice on exercising her stock options and then what to do with them. The first thing I asked was if I could tell her how to avoid losing 50 per cent of her assets overnight. She said, "Yes, of course!" I told her to get a marital agreement in place before she says "I do." I referred her to a wonderful family lawyer to talk about how she could set up a fair agreement that would lay things out clearly and fairly between them. I explained that this lawyer really is a romantic at heart and is gifted at mediating and holding the values of the couple. The woman wouldn't go. She married him. She didn't become a client either. Maybe she will come back later, when he takes off with a younger woman and half the cash.

Does that sound cynical? I hope not. I am just constantly flabbergasted by women's romantic notions about the business of marriage and their fear that asking for an above-board discussion of what is fair and what they each expect will result in rejection.

UN-PARTNERING CAN mean divorce, the death of a loved one or simply moving out. There are strong emotional and financial currents running through these situations that are most often highly stressful. These difficult life changes are made even worse if a woman has been asleep financially during the relationship. They can experience rage, grief, depression, deep shame and self-loathing. It's not easy. The same process that goes into financial planning is replicated in separation planning. All five steps get covered, just with two scenarios: together and apart.

The benefit of un-partnering is that people who have been disempowered in their relationships begin to regain their independence and autonomy. It can be both scary and exhilarating. Divorcing women are our most motivated clients. They care, they are awakened and they want to know. Now. It is actually an emancipating and exciting period in their financial lives, punctuated by terror. Great progress is made. I have been known to say that divorcing women could take over the world, because they have stepped into their full power and are financially awake. It's just unfortunate that the knowledge has had to come at such a high price. But it doesn't have to be that way.

This is one of the key stages where women talk a lot about real estate. They want to know if they can keep their home and, if not, whether they should buy or rent. There are no easy answers. Lots of numbers get run. The answer depends on how much you pay in rent, how well positioned you are to take on a mortgage, what your salary level is and your age. It can also depend on your geographic location and the opportunities and challenges of that city. You will need help from professionals to make a thorough evaluation of this question.

RETIREMENT

There are many stages of adulthood, and these lead into retirement. Although conventional thought is that retirement is something that happens when you are old, it's actually what happens when you no longer have to work for your money. This is the point of financial independence. You have saved and worked and invested and planned, and now you are at the crossroad, where the capital you have accumulated or the income streams you have established will carry you either fully or partially through your lifetime without having to work.

I actually don't even believe in retirement, in conventional terms. Most of us just want to go from working for our money to having our money work for us. That can happen at 60, or 40, or even 90. It doesn't mean you have to quit your job, just that you could if you chose to. Or you could work in a different way. I actually prefer that people work at something that makes them happy whenever possible, and I'm sure they prefer it too.

The number one issue I see facing the retirees I work with is depression. In our practise, we end up sending people back to work so that they won't go crazy. We're not meant to sit around for 35 years. We need to be engaged, to be essential to someone or something, for our mental and physical well-being. In short, we need to shift the way we think about this stage in life.

Although retirement isn't a term I like, I use it because it is the term most commonly used (if poorly understood). It's generally and erroneously thought to be a finite, time-limited old person's experience. In reality, it's a series of phases along the adult development continuum, and they are much more complex and demand more active management now than they did for our parents. We're healthier and are living longer. There's a potential to have 30 or even 40 years of healthy living after we stop working full time. It affects everything: how we manage our careers, how we retire, what we invest in. Everything.

At Sophia, we have identified four main developmental stages at the far end of the aging continuum that we call the Four Phases of Retirement.

Phase one: *Productive Engagement*

This is a multi-faceted period when, having left our primary life occupation, either we choose different work or we work at our careers in a different way. It's a form of quasi-retirement, where business people pass ownership or power to other people in their company to succeed them. Or instead of working five days a week, they cut down to two to three days a week. We can be 50 or 78 at this point. We work in mentorship roles or consulting or in leadership roles in our companies, organizations and professions. The underlying principle is that some degree of creativity is applied to how money is earned.

Many of our clients begin new businesses in this phase. Others run for political office or take on substantial roles in volunteer organizations. This is not the old-fashioned version of retirement, where a grey-haired, bright-eyed geezer rocks away on a porch, drinking iced tea or playing cribbage.

This phase often brings an improvement in quality of life, because stress is reduced when the need to work every day is eliminated or lessened. Financially, you're still in the world. You're still making money and conducting business. And yet the pressure is off. You will tend to be spending the same amount of money as you always have, but because income is still coming in, you will be drawing less from your savings than in later years. This is a time for finishing up the work that is left undone in your career while still bringing in money.

Sometimes people retrain during this stage. They become dog walkers, floral designers or social activists. They find an answer to the question "What do you want to be when you grow up?" or make peace with not having done so. You can look after your grandkids, you can sell jam out of your basement, you can be a career counsellor. But in this phase, you are productive in ways that bring you joy and satisfaction.

When I suggest to women in their sixties or seventies that they return to work, they always think no one is going to hire them. The truth is quite the opposite. Employers are starved for workers who come in on time, are respectful and don't text or tweet every five minutes, and the mature women are snapped up in a heartbeat.

Phase two: Kilimanjaro

This phase is expensive. People do the things they've wanted to do their whole lives. They unearth their long-buried dreams. In this phase, you're at the point where you think about the things or people you want to experience. It might be "I want to date an Irishman—in Ireland!" or "I want to climb Kilimanjaro."

Health and vitality, energy and mobility are high. You have an agenda, and you feel a certain sense of urgency in wanting to achieve your dreams. These longings can be life changing when acted upon. I have seen couples regenerate their marriages after doing volunteer work overseas and women taking on young lovers while biking through French vineyards. I have known people to take courses at universities, travel to parts of the world to which they've never been and run marathons. This stage looks like a lot of fun and can be much more expensive than any other stage of life so far.

Phase three: Home Is Where the Heart Is

You're tuckered out, you've seen or done what you want to in life. Now you're ready to focus on and take care of your home-based needs. This phase is the least expensive of all the adult phases and much less expensive than the Kilimanjaro phase. Health is good and the thirst for adventure has abated. There is a calm settling in this stage of life. Important goals have been achieved, or peace has been made with not achieving them. Activities like gardening, learning languages, running for city office and playing bridge are rewarding.

Phase four: Living In Community

At this point, by choice or necessity, you no longer want to live independently. You want to be with others, or you may simply need assistance of some kind to function optimally. This phase can last months, or years, and is often quite expensive, depending on how much assistance is required. This is also when your home can be liquidated to provide a kind of long-term care fund (if you are in a high-priced real estate market like Vancouver or New York), or you call on larger savings or insurance to fund it.

This is also the time when gender differences re-emerge. With men often predeceasing their wives, the woman has done the lion's share of caring and domestic upkeep during his last phase of life. When it comes time for *her* to require help, it is the younger family members who have to step in or purchase the services needed to maintain a satisfactory and safe daily life. This is an issue that we try to plan for early on. We have had to force this reality into many couples' awareness, because the money they were taking out of retirement savings and pensions is fine to get them through his lifetime, but not enough would be left over for hers. If you add the seven or eight years women generally outlive men, with the five-to-seven-year age difference that is common (another good reason for women to partner with younger men!), a woman can be left managing declining health and mobility for quite a while on her own.

We've learned that each phase of retirement has a different income need, so each one is going to have a different-looking portfolio. The architecture of a retirement plan is the same as any other financial plan. Cash flow is now thought of as "income streams," like your expected Canada Pension Plan (CPP) monthly payments, Old Age Security (OAS), pension from work, dividends, rental properties, spousal support, money from a company business or trust. Each stream of income may have a different tax consequence, so it is easier if you look at the numbers *after* taxes when you are designing your cash flow for the different retirement phases.

So many of the assumptions about retirement planning view income needs as being reduced during these years, but as you can see from our four phases, they vary depending on the person and the dreams. We've never had a situation where a client has wanted us to do calculations for a *lower* standard of living for their retirement—they want to continue living the same way they do now, or better. They like their lifestyle or they wouldn't be living that way.

The other big factor in doing projections is that we can't accurately predict anyone's life expectancy. This is the most critical number and the one that is never really known until it no longer matters. We make educated guesses and get all huffy about numbers that in our minds are too conservative or liberal. The fact is, we really just don't know.

Retirement is now too long of a period to allocate your money back to cash or gold bars. Old adages about calculating your fixed income allocation according to your age are simplistic and ageist. We do have to accept, though, that some of these calculations are complicated because the cumulative effects of inflation and changing rates of return can be hard to measure.

In simple terms, a person says: "I need $2,000 per month to live on." We look at what they're receiving already. "I have $1,500 guaranteed monthly through the municipal pension." They just need an extra $500 per month.

Then we look at how much capital (savings) they need in order to draw that out for the number of specified years (for example, from 60 to 95) and then we run the numbers. If the numbers don't quite work, there are numerous options. They may be able to work longer, lower their expenses, die early (usually not a preferred solution) or take on more volatility in their portfolios. We essentially calculate numbers to the "enough" figure, and that's the first step towards peace of mind and being in control.

Ironically, the less money a woman has, the more volatility she may need to have in her portfolio. It runs directly counter to our instincts. Normally, the more nervous we are, the more we want to avoid any threat of loss or volatility. We want to avoid it, and yet it may be the only way to get a rate of return that will meet our goals.

In each stage of retirement, we like to have a "cash bucket." This is in *addition* to cash reserve. It is typically anywhere from one to three years of income, set aside from the portfolio. Then we might have another portfolio that is an asset allocation of either 50/50 (stocks to bonds) or 60/40 to run for the next five to ten years. Then another portfolio for long-term needs. We might go 80/20 in the long-term investments, since this timeline could be 20 or 30 years long. We regularly harvest positive returns by moving these gains from a long-term portfolio to a shorter one. This helps us ensure stability of income and allows the market time to make us money.

I often have young women write letters from the perspective of their 90-year-old selves to the younger woman they are today. It is a very meaningful exercise, because a life expectancy that stretches to 94 is very hard to conceive of, and yet we need to have a personal relationship with that future self. We are her best friend right *now*. The more real her needs are to us now, the better able we will be to protect her and make the decisions today that will support her security in a distant reality. Interestingly, my younger clients easily let me put in 94 or 100 for life expectancy calculations, but my older clients fight me on it. "I don't want to live that long!" many of them say. It is a difficult concept to get your head around if you have always thought of 94 as decrepit and drooling. But think of Sally from the empowered investing classes I spoke about in Chapter 2 if you ever want to project a more positive image of what 94 can be: growing, learning, laughing—and still dating!

ESTATE AND LEGACY PLANNING

When we're young, we don't talk about end-stage planning. We have our kids, and we know what we're going to be doing for the next 22 and a half years. We're friends with other women and have open dialogues about our lives, probably dozens of times over the course of a day, without even trying. But when we're in our seventies and our children have grown and those networks of people aren't as easy to connect with anymore, we have to become very intentional—much more so than before. This period has to have more purpose and intention than any other period of our lives.

I want to mention that since moving back to Vancouver I've only had two clients who wanted to leave money to their kids. The generation that is currently dying off is leaving significant legacies of wealth to the baby boomer generation. It is the boomers who want to spend it all, rather than pass it on. I think that trend is going to have serious repercussions. If you're counting on Aunt Betsy to leave you enough money to pay off your mortgage, you may want to think again.

One of the areas in which you will need professional advice is in the area of wills, estate and representation agreements, and legacy planning.

Using an estate planning lawyer is something a woman will have to do more than once in her lifetime. At each stage of life, different legal protective gestures are needed. As we move along our financial and life journey, our circumstances change as a result of marriage, death, divorce, the birth of children and grandchildren, mental or physical illness and increasing (or decreasing) wealth. We will need to revisit our needs.

A representation agreement and a personal directive may not be as important to a 25-year-old woman as they would be for a woman who is 65. However, a 65-year-old woman will not need to worry about a guardian for her children if her life ends, but a 25-year-old with young children will need to address this possibility or risk having her children become wards of the court.

We also want to be alert to changes in the law that may affect our current written intentions. If we don't keep our plan up to date, it could mean an ex-spouse or some other undesirable person will become the beneficiary of our estate. Or it could mean, in the event of our death or disability, that our children are cared for by someone we can't stand, or worse, that they become wards of the court (a scenario that is only appealing when they are teenagers and we are still alive.)

With advances in medicine, illnesses and conditions that used to be fatal can now allow for a long life, but one that is fraught with significant physical and mental challenges. Without a written document, you could receive life-saving medical care that leaves you with no quality of life when you would have chosen to pass on. You want to make sure that if a time comes when you cannot speak for yourself, you will get (or not get) the kind of care and treatment that you would have asked for. It also means that family, loved ones and health care providers will not be struggling to find those answers at a time of crisis. When it happens that a woman never got around to addressing her own estate planning needs, and documents have not been properly prepared, it can cause irreparable damage to relationships between family members and loved ones. You remember how you and your siblings fought over the TV remote; just imagine that disagreement taking place over whether to "pull the plug" or keep you on life support.

13

A CARE PACKAGE
FOR THE ROAD

////////////////////////

W**E ARE** now in the last leg of our journey together. I feel like a character in one of those old movies where the one left behind is running alongside a departing train calling out their last admonishments or declarations of love to a passenger whose nose is pressed against the window.

I am sad to see our time together coming to an end, but I also can't let you go until I am sure you have what you need to move ahead confidently. So, I am going to wrap up a few tools and words of encouragement and toss them to you as the train goes chugging off, returning you to your life.

T**HE PRINCIPLES** of this book are that:

1. Women and men are different...for better and for worse.
2. We are all on a journey from somewhere to somewhere else on the wealth continuum. Wherever that may be, there is always a next step that we can take to move ahead. And there is always hope. One step is enough.
3. There are three basic areas that together make up our financial identity, and they are in the psychological, educational and behavioural realms.

4. There are five steps in financial planning. Regardless of where you are on the wealth continuum, your gender, your age or stage of life, this architecture applies.

5. You are not alone. And you can't achieve your financial goals alone. So, it all works out. The phrase "We are all alone in this together" is apt.

6. The world of money is made up of stories. Stories of catastrophe, illumination, bullshit and revelation. There are stories we tell ourselves and each other, and stories the media tells us. Our job is to own our own lives so that we can identify and pay special attention to the stories that lift us up and learn to ignore the others.

7. There will always be "trouble at the border." It is not a sign to turn back but a confirmation that you are about to break through to a new level.

8. Recognize what is in your control and what isn't. Master what is, and let go of what isn't.

9. Beware of fussing: It is the drug of choice for the insecure. Beware of self-deprecation: It is the drug of choice for the frustrated. Beware of hopelessness: It is the drug of choice for those with unacknowledged power.

10. All is well. You are enough. It is what it is. So be it.

THERE IS a story I used to tell in my classes. I read it in *Women Who Run with the Wolves: Myths and Stories of the Wild Woman Archetype* by Clarissa Pinkola Estés, who heard it from her late Uncle Vilmos.

It tells the story of a man who goes to a tailor to buy a suit. He tries one on and is standing in front of the mirror when he notices that the vest is a little uneven at the bottom. The tailor assures him that this is a minor issue and not worth worrying about. He instructs him to just tug down the corner with his left hand, assuring him that it will be fine. The man makes the adjustment then sees that the collar is also flawed. It seems to curl a bit at one corner. Again, the tailor dismisses his concern and explains that with a simple little chin movement the corner can be held in place. The customer then notices that the trouser inseam is uneven and tight on one side. The tailor shows him how to pull it down with his right hand to make the problem less noticeable. The customer complies with these instructions and buys the suit.

The next day the man hobbles across the park, contorted by all the alterations necessary to make his new suit look decent. With his chin holding the collar down, one hand tugging his inseam and the other hand pulling at the vest, he limps past two men playing checkers. They look up to see the man making his way awkwardly across the grounds and whisper words of pity to each other. "That poor handicapped man," one man says, shaking his head in sympathy. "Yes," the other man replies, "but what a great looking suit!"

The women in my classes can always relate to this story. They know what it is like to get bad advice—and then take it. They know the cost of presenting a good front and the pain that comes from contorting themselves to sustain it. And they understand its relevance to money. It is very hard to admit that you have been walking around getting approval and being so nice to look at but failing at managing your own life. It is heartbreaking to realize that people do pay attention to what is on the outside and not what is tearing you up on the inside. We know it. This story rarely even gets a laugh. It is funny only in that we recognize ourselves. It is also not funny, for the same reason.

I think we are ready to let go of our crotches and lift our chins up and face our reality. Our pants may fall off. Those watching us may gasp in dismay or disapproval, and if it comes to this, I say to you: So what? So. What. We are not bombing parliament or beating our children. We are looking our financial lives square in the eyes and taking stock. We are looking into our hearts and seeing what makes us tick. We are asking the questions. So many questions. The ones we are learning to ask. The dumb questions (yes, there are dumb questions, but who cares?!), the hard questions and the can't-quite-find-the-right-words questions. We are listening to the answers and then asking for more information. We are taking notes, sometimes disagreeing and asking for clarification.

We are acknowledging that the men in our lives do not innately know more than we do, that our cultural paradigm blinds us to our own intelligence and wisdom about economics. We are a voice of balance and compassion and sustainability. We are mastering our financial lives not just for ourselves, our kids and our communities but for the world at large. We are necessary in this world. Our perspective and desire for context is essential.

We will also learn from the masculine. Men make decisions more efficiently, and we could emulate some of those cognitive short cuts. They don't take dissension and disagreement personally. They assume they are smart and that they know what they are doing. Men assume they are responsible for the money. They assume the world is for them, not against them. Men are rarely hopeless about a salary negotiation before it even begins, and they apply for jobs before they are fully qualified. They expect others to pick up after them and to be obeyed. Not a bad gig.

We are not playing at being men, blaming men or even idolizing them. We are attempting to stay whole in our femaleness and to take the qualities that will work for us from the man buffet. We want the wisdom of both genders to coexist peacefully inside us. We can find a balanced path that leads us to the life we want. We can feel financially empowered with grace and ease as women.

We can attain all the money knowledge that we need to achieve our destiny. And we will make a decent hospital corner and wipe the nose of a child at our knee while we do it. We can do it because we are centred in ourselves and in our own lives, and because we have each other.

And that's pretty much everything we really want to know about money.

GLOSSARY

Asset Something that is owned. It has financial value and could be converted into cash now or in the future. It can be something tangible, like a home or diamonds, or intangible, like the formula for Mrs. Fields's cookies or the goodwill in a business.

Asset Class A way of sorting assets into categories that have similar characteristics and risk levels. There are three primary asset classes: cash, fixed income (bonds) and equities (stocks). There are also many other kinds of assets, and they are often grouped together as alternative asset classes. Examples of these are precious metals, art or hedge funds. Most often real estate is classified as an asset class as well.

Asset Allocation The process of sorting and assigning investments into categories in an attempt to balance volatility and reward (return) by adjusting the percentage of each asset class in an investment portfolio according to an investor's risk tolerance, goals and investment time frame. If a person needs to save for a goal that is 20 years away, they may have a greater percentage of stocks to bonds and cash (like 70 per cent equity,

25 per cent bond and 5 per cent cash). If they are saving for a down payment on a house and want the money in five years, they want a different allocation, like 50 per cent stocks, 30 per cent bond, 20 per cent cash. Each class has, in the past, produced a characteristic rate of return and a level of volatility. This general framework is created by allocating assets even before investments are chosen. It is like planning a meal. You decide you want a meat, a starch and two vegetables because together they produce the balance of nutrition or outcome you want. Then you choose what kind of meat or starch. You might hear language like 60-40 or 90-10, and this is generally the ratio of equity to bonds in a portfolio.

Bond A "fixed income security" offered by governments and businesses. You lend them money for a set period of time in return for interest that they pay you for the privilege of having your money for that time period. The rate of interest depends on the credit rating of the issuer (the one who borrowed your money) at the time of the bond issue. For example, the interest rate will be higher if there is a greater risk of them not paying you back your principal at the end of the term. This is called "defaulting." There are many kinds of bonds and thousands of issuers, all with different credit ratings. Loan durations typically run from 1 to 30 years. You will find higher interest rates for longer durations because the company's ability to pay may change radically the longer the time the bond is out.

Broker Dealer A firm in the business of buying and selling securities, operating as both a broker and a dealer, depending on the transaction. Membership in IIROC (Investment Industry Regulatory Organization of Canada) is mandatory for any firm wishing to operate as a securities dealer in Canada. Retail firms include full service firms and discount brokers. Full service retail firms offer a wide variety of products and services for the retail investor. Discount brokers execute trades over the telephone and the Internet for clients at reduced rates but don't provide advice. An investment or financial advisor who wants to be able to offer stocks or bonds in the portfolios they design for clients must have a licence held by a broker dealer.

Capital Gains/Growth
An increase in the value of an investment (a capital asset). The difference between the purchase price and the sales price is positive, and this represents your gain in capital. A gain is not realized until the asset is sold. A capital gain must be claimed on income taxes.

Cash Money under your mattress or in a bank or financial institution. Currency in the form of banknotes or coins.

Cash Equivalents Can be converted to cash quickly. Instruments that act like cash are considered "liquid," meaning they can be easily and immediately bought or sold or used as currency. Examples of cash equivalents are: money market funds, term deposits, GICS (Guaranteed Investment Certificates) and treasury bills. They are very low risk and typically offer low interest rates.

Cash Flow Money in minus money out. Positive cash flow is when there is more money coming in than going out, and it is negative when there is more money going out than coming in.

CFP-Certified Financial Planner Financial planning is not regulated in most Canadian provinces. This means that anyone can call themselves a financial planner, but not everyone who refers to themselves as a planner is qualified. Many are licensed to sell products but have no financial planning training or expertise. The CFP is a designation that is considered the gold standard for Canada. It requires taking and passing two days of exams, years of industry experience and ongoing stringent continuing education to maintain certification.

Financial Planning A process that determines how you can best meet your life goals through the proper management of your financial affairs. The key to effective financial planning is the ability to take into account all relevant aspects of your financial situation, understand the lay of the land and identify and analyze the relationships among objectives, resources and challenges.

Currency A medium of exchange. It can be love, marbles, chocolate or approval, but for the purposes of this book, unless otherwise specified, it is money.

Diversification The practise of spreading money among different investments to reduce risk. By choosing a variety of different asset classes or different countries or different sectors, you may be able to limit your losses and reduce the fluctuations of investment returns without sacrificing too much potential gain. The goal is to reduce the losses that come from having "too many eggs in one basket" and reduce the ups and downs in value of a portfolio—reduce volatility as well as increase the rate of return. Different asset classes and investments go up and down at different times and for different reasons. Example: When my son was experiencing serious medical challenges as a child, every doctor proposed a new diet. Some wanted him off of wheat, some off dairy, some wanted him on grains and off meat and on it went. I eventually varied his diet and allowed him a food group every four days. This allowed him the benefits of the vitamins and minerals of the different food groups while minimizing overexposure to any one to a degree that might harm him or stir an allergic reaction.

Dividends A dividend is a distribution of profits that a corporation makes to its shareholders (the people who own stocks in that company). A dividend is paid as a set amount for each share of stock the shareholder owns.

Equity An ownership stake in something. With your house, it's the part that you (and not the bank) actually own outright. In investing, an equity is a stock or share of a company. When you become a partial owner of a company, you get a share of the profits in the form of dividends. You also participate in its growth. In common terms, we talk about the ratio of equity to fixed income, and this is the portion that is stocks versus bonds.

ETF (Exchange Traded Fund) A fund that holds the same mix of investments (or securities) that are in a particular index, like the S&P/TSX 60 or the Dow Jones. Its mandate is to follow or track that index with little to no intervention from a manager. It is attractive because it has lower fees than a traditional mutual fund.

Fixed Income A phrase often confused with "pension." It's used interchangeably with the term "bonds," where you are lending your money to a company or government for a set period of time for an agreed-upon interest rate. When the time ends, it is called the "bond's maturity date"—when the company or government that borrowed your money is supposed to pay it back in full.

IIROC (Investment Industry Regulatory Organization of Canada) The national regulatory organization that oversees all investment dealers (broker dealers) and all the trading in the debt (bonds) and equity (stocks) markets in Canada. It sets standards of care, protects investors and has a mandate to strengthen market integrity (the public trust of it) so that it can maintain efficient and competitive markets for participants. The NHL of the investing world.

Index Indexes allow us to track groups of securities or instruments like stocks, bonds and commodities, as a whole instead of simply following an individual stock or bond. How the whole group performs in a particular segment. Provides an overview and also allows comparison of a single part to the whole. Just as you can't really gauge the health of a garden from a single plant; you can't gauge the performance of the market from the performance of a single security.

Liability What we owe. An obligation that binds us to pay someone else for a debt.

MER (Management Expense Ratio) The total of the management fees and operating expenses of a mutual fund. Includes fees paid to advisors for the service they provide to clients buying the funds, bookkeeping and administrative fees, filings with the provincial securities commissions, legal fees, audit fees and the fees of researchers and managers of the fund.

MFDA (Mutual Fund Dealers Association of Canada) Another national self-regulatory organization that regulates the operations, standards of practise and business conduct of members of the mutual fund industry.

Mutual Fund A pool of investments. Allows you to hold a portion of many more investments than you could normally purchase on your own. They are managed by professional portfolio managers and allow you to diversify your portfolio with potentially less of an investment than if you had to purchase each security on its own. The investor actually holds a portion, called a unit, and the price of the units goes up and down based on the value of the investments inside the fund. You can (but you don't have to) redeem a mutual fund at the end of each trading day.

Net Worth Assets minus liabilities—what you own minus what you owe.

RESP (Registered Education Savings Plan) A tax-sheltered account used to save for children's education.

RRSP (Registered Retirement Savings Plan) Lets you save and invest for retirement. It is registered with the government and allows you to reduce the income tax you pay at the time of contribution. You do not pay taxes on it until it is withdrawn. You place investments into an RRSP. It's not an investment itself but the container that investments go into.

RRIF (Registered Retirement Income Fund) Registered fund with Canada Revenue Agency (like the RRSP.) You transfer holdings into it from your RRSP or other Registered Pension Plan to generate income from your retirement plans. Establishing a RRIF can be done at any time but must be done no later than the year the investor turns 71. Once a RRIF is established, there can be no more contributions made to the plan.

Risk A measure of the amount of uncertainty about the expected return of an investment. In financial terms, it is *not* a measure of the possibility that an investment might lose money or become worthless. It is the variance of that investment in comparison to the average performance of the other investments of its type. In theory, an investment can be considered high risk even if it outperformed the other instruments of its class.

Risk Tolerance Looks at acceptable/unacceptable deviations from what is expected. "Risk appetite" looks at how much risk one is willing to accept. Risk tolerance is now used in everyday language to mean risk appetite—an individual's emotional response to uncertainty.

Securities A financial instrument with value that represents ownership.

Stock Pieces of ownership in a company, also known as shares or equities. You can receive dividends and/or capital growth from that company. The value of your stock will rise and fall according to the value the market places on the health and growth of the company.

Stockbroker An antiquated term for a financial professional who is licensed (by IIROC) to buy and sell stocks and bonds. They must have an affiliation with a broker dealer. Currently known as investment representatives, investment advisors, portfolio managers, financial advisors and financial consultants.

TFSA (Tax-Free Savings Account) Allows Canadians age 18 and over to set money aside tax-free throughout their lifetime. Each calendar year, you can contribute up to that year's limit (in 2013 it is $5,500), any unused TFSA contribution room from the previous year and the amount you withdrew the year before. All money earned and withdrawals made from a TFSA are tax-free. Having a TFSA does not affect federal benefits and credits.

TSX (Toronto Stock Exchange, formerly TSE) Largest stock exchange in Canada, the third largest in North America and the seventh largest in the world by market capitalization. On October 25, 1861, 24 men gathered at the Masonic Hall to officially create the Toronto Stock Exchange. A broad range of businesses from Canada, the United States, Europe and other countries are represented on the exchange. More mining and oil and gas companies are listed on Toronto Stock Exchange than any other exchange in the world.

Volatility Refers to the amount of uncertainty or risk about the size of changes in a security's value. Higher volatility means that the price of the security can change dramatically in either direction, over a short time period. Lower volatility means that a security's value doesn't fluctuate dramatically but changes in value at a steady pace over a period of time. There is a correlation between volatility and the potential for reward, meaning that investors can be well compensated for enduring large ups and downs in an investment by getting greater returns.

ABOUT
SOPHIA FINANCIAL GROUP

////////////////////

SOPHIA FINANCIAL GROUP is a full-service financial advisory firm affiliated with Raymond James and located in Vancouver, B.C. We provide financial planning, investment strategy and portfolio management services. We typically work with people with over half a million dollars in investable assets.

We are financial planners, and that means we hold the CFP (Certified Financial Planner) designation. We are also stockbrokers, which means we are licensed by the government's securities commission (IIROC) to sell equity, stocks and bonds—all of the financial instruments in the debt and equity markets approved by our broker dealer. We are insurance licensed and financial divorce specialists and are also both Fellows of the Canadian Securities Institute.

At Sophia, we believe in education and more education. We want people to understand their financial world and to feel confident and empowered. One of our central undertakings is a day-long workshop for women called Sophia Wealth Academy: Everything a Woman Wants to Know About Her Finances in One Day (www.sophiawealthacademy.com).

At Wealth Academy, we bring in the best and brightest experts in Vancouver to talk about debt, gender, career strategy, banking, negotiation, investing, the psychology of wealth and financial planning processes. We have run it seven times now, and each year it gets bigger and more exhilarating. All proceeds raised have gone to Dress for Success, an organization devoted to women becoming and staying self-sufficient.

The room is filled with women from all walks of life and financial circumstances. A woman who has just been "off the streets" for three weeks trying to find new work may be sitting beside a multi-millionaire. A new university graduate may be in a group with an 80-year-old widow. Magic happens. Our investment classes and education programs are at the heart of our work and express our passion for sharing knowledge that empowers.

We pair education with collaboration. Not only do we want people to have appropriate strategies, but we want to work with our clients as partners with full transparency. We believe that our five-step financial planning process is unique, efficient and comprehensive. We call it the Sophia Way.

A first meeting at Sophia is about an hour long. We find out what brought you here, what your life is like and what keeps you up at night. We discuss your values and goals, who you care about and your background. We ask and answer lots of questions to gather the preliminary information we need to create a complete financial picture.

In our second meeting, we use that background information and the financial data to crunch the numbers. Our analysis can take anywhere from four to ten hours, with the explanation and discussion taking about 90 minutes. We may be looking at the numbers to answer more complex, quite specific questions like "Can I retire in three years and still take $2,000 a month from my retirement investments?" or "Can I travel the world for the next three years, or will that affect my ability to sell my business for the amount I want to?"

The next step is the proposal generation. This maps out the details of the most effective strategy options. These strategies pull together financial data, objectives, the cost involved in the various scenarios and the various risk levels. At any point we might refer you to a counsellor, lawyer, accountant or your bank to get more information.

The fourth step is chiseling out the operational details and action steps that need to be taken after the strategy has been decided on. We spell out various tasks like what parts of a business need to be sold, what gets transferred or what financial products need to be purchased. Then we begin implementing the best of these solutions.

The last step is to collaborate on how we will evaluate your progress and monitor the plan. We set up the next session to teach you how to interpret the financial and reporting documents you will receive. Then we talk about how we will keep in touch, when we will see each other next and under what conditions we will make contact.

The client-advisor relationship is a dynamic journey along which money is brought into alignment with life's ins and outs, ups and downs. Its purpose is to facilitate financial harmony and success, in which your money serves your life and not the other way around.

See sophiafinancial.ca.

REFERENCES

Babcock, Linda; Laschever, Sara: *Women Don't Ask: The High Cost of Avoiding Negotiation—and Positive Strategies for Change*, (2007) Bantam Dell, NY, NY.

Barletta, Marti: *Marketing to Women: How to Understand, Reach, and Increase Your Share of the World's Largest Market Segment*, 2nd Edition, (2006) Dearborn Trade Publishing, Chicago, IL.

Baron-Cohen, Simon: *The Essential Difference: Male and Female Brains and the Truth About Autism*, (2003) Basic Books, NY.

Caranci, Beata and Gauthier, Pascal: *Career Interrupted: The Economic Impact of Motherhood*, (October 12, 2010) TD Economics Special Report.

Dehaas, Josh: "Women Graduates Expect to Make Less Money," (May 19, 2011) macleans.ca.

Estroff Marano, Hara: "The New Sex Scorecard: Men's and Women's Minds Really Do Work Differently—But Not On Everything" (July 1, 2003) *Psychology Today.*

Golman, Daniel: *Social Intelligence: The New Science of Human Relationships*, (2007) Bantam Books, NY, NY.

Grant, Tavia: "Financial Security 'Elusive' for Many Canadian Families," (March 22, 2012) globeandmail.com.

Gysler, Matthias, Kruse, Jamie and Schubert, Renate: Ambiguity and Gender Differences in Financial Decision Making—An Experimental Examination of Competence and Confidence Effects, Swiss Federal Institute of Technology, (2002) Center for Economic Research.

IIROC Investment Industry Regulatory Organization of Canada, Investor Education Pages, How to Invest.

Meyers-Levy, J.: "Gender Differences in Information Processing: A Selectivity Interpretation," in *Cognitive and Affective Responses to Advertising*, P. Cafferata and A. Tybout (eds.), (1988) Lexington Books, Lanham, MD.

Meyers-Levy, J., and D. Maheswaran: "Exploring Males' and Females' Processing Strategies: When and Why Do Differences Occur in Consumers' Processing of Ad Claims," *Journal of Consumer Research*, (1991).

Perkins Gilman, Charlotte: *Women and Economics—A Study of the Economic Relation Between Men and Women as a Factor in Social Evolution*, (1898) Cosimo Publications, NY, NY.

Pinkola Estes, Clarissa: *Women Who Run with the Wolves*, (1995) Random House, NY, NY.

Rosener, Judy B.: "Leadership and the Paradox of Gender," in *Women, Men and Gender*, ed. Mary Ruth Walsh, (1997) Yale University Press, New Haven, CT.

Stanny, Barbara: *Prince Charming Isn't Coming: How Women Get Smart About Money*, (1997) Penguin Group, NY, NY.

Stewart, Barbara: "Financial Lives of Girls and Women," (white paper), (2010).

Tannen, Deborah: *That's Not What I Meant!: How Conversational Style Makes or Breaks Relationships*, (2011) Harper Collins, NY, NY.

Twist, Lynn: *The Soul of Money*, (2003) WW Norton and Co., NY, NY.

Thomas Yaccato, Joanne: *The 80% Minority: Reaching the Real World of Women Consumers*, (2004) Penguin Group, Toronto, ON.

PROFESSIONAL
ACKNOWLEDGMENTS

///////////////////////

SPECIAL THANKS to the following professionals who contributed their valuable insights and input to Chapter 11:

Sony Baron, MA, MA, RCC, baroncounselling.com

Kamal Basra, CFP, FCSI, sophiafinancial.ca

Bettyanne Brownlee, Barrister and Solicitor, pinnaclelaw.ca

Marci Deane, Mortgage Broker, askmarci.ca

Marlene Delanghe, MA, career-solutions.ca

Angiola-Patrizia De Stefanis, JD, Alliance Lex Law Corporation, alliancelex.com

Carrie Gallant, JD, gallantsolutionsinc.com

Lana Gilbertson, CIRP, Trustee, Senior. VP, MNP, mnpdebt.ca

Nicola McLaren, CA, nicolamclaren.ca

Karin Mizgala, MBA, CFP, moneycoachescanada.ca

Corinne Schindler, Mortgage Specialist, RBC, mortgages.rbcroyalbank.com

Sheila Walkington, CFP, moneycoachescanada.ca